the complete guide to

buying property in Spain

charles davey

KOGAN
PAGE

London and Sterling, VA

First published in Great Britain in 2004

Kogan Page Limited
120 Pentonville Road
London N1 9JN
United Kingdom
www.kogan-page.co.uk

Kogan Page US
22883 Quicksilver Drive
Sterling VA 20166–2012
USA

© Charles Davey, 2004

British Library Cataloguing-in-Publication Data

A CIP record for this book is available from the British Library.

ISBN 0 7494 4056 2

Typeset by Saxon Graphics Ltd, Derby
Printed and bound in Great Britain by Thanet Press Ltd, Margate

Contents

Contents

Preface

Glorious Spain! With ever-increasing numbers of low-cost flights to Spanish locations, the number of Britons purchasing a holiday home in Spain or emigrating there shows no signs of a downturn. According to the Spanish central bank, the amount spent by foreign nationals (mostly British and German) on real estate transactions in Spain from January to August 2003 rose by 24.9 per cent compared to the previous year.

Those who have purchased already have seen rapid growth in the value of their properties. A recent report in the *Economist* claimed that in the period 1995–2002 house prices in Spain rose at three times the average across the Eurozone, fuelled not only by the foreign property buyer, but also by the fastest growing economy in Europe. The increase has been most marked in the last four years or so, with a surge of 15 per cent a year on average since 1998. The Banco Bilbao Vizcaya Argentaria has predicted prices for 2004 will rise by 17 per cent.

Despite steep rises in property prices, however, Spain is still very much 'good value' when it comes to buying a home. Furthermore, even after taking into account the rises in the value of the euro against the pound, prices of consumer goods, for example, remain about 10 per cent lower than in the UK, with food and clothes being also generally cheaper. The interest of foreign buyers in the Spanish property market remains high, with the amount spent last year on Spanish real estate staying well ahead of the increase in property prices.

It is all too easy, however, to fall into the trap that as Spain is a European country, and has undergone rapid development in the last 30 years, the rules and regulations governing property purchases mirror those in the UK. This is not the case. There are certain rules, regulations and practices that the prospective buyer should be aware of. Only by knowing and adhering to these can you be best protected against a purchase that could ultimately result in serious financial losses and possibly costly, lengthy and difficult court proceedings. The peaceful holiday or retirement home or, worse still, your principal residence, could turn into a veritable nightmare.

Anyone contemplating buying a house or home in Spain needs to have a basic knowledge of the process. I have endeavoured to give a precise step-by-step guide in understandable English for the prospective purchaser. I use the legal terminology in both English and Spanish with a clear explanation of the meanings of terms used throughout the book to make the information here accessible to all.

As a practising barrister, I am familiar with advising clients after a disaster has occurred. It is my hope and intention to guide the prospective purchaser away from the pitfalls ahead so that this situation does not occur. To this end I have placed the emphasis very much on practical advice and guidance.

This book deals with the nitty-gritty of buying or renting a home in Spain, and provides practical advice on living in Spain. It is designed to guide you through the legal labyrinth of jargon, and the general information necessary for the prospective purchaser. It is not a book about Spanish culture or history, or about the delights of living in Spain. Rather, this book concentrates on the important aspects of acquiring a home in Spain, on the practical issues pertinent to purchasing and renting a property, and settling in Spain. Where other books advise a particular course of action (such as renting before you buy), this book goes one step further by telling you how to do it.

This book aims to guide you through the main issues to help facilitate your acquisition of a house in Spain, how to make your home there, and how to avoid the mistakes that others have made.

Acknowledgements

My grateful thanks to everyone at Kogan Page who has helped bring this book to publication. I would especially like to express my appreciation to Jon Finch, Commissioning Editor, for his constructive comments and professional advice.

Lastly I would like to thank my wife Michaela, whom I have had the good fortune to have as my closest friend as well as my wife, without whose constant support and encouragement this book would never have been written.

SPAIN: COSTAS, MOUNTAINS AND MAIN CITIES

1 Choosing your location

Once you have decided to move to Spain or to buy a holiday or retirement home there, the next decision is to choose an area. There is a wide diversity and considerable care is required before coming to a decision. Although property prices are generally much lower in Spain than in the UK, the costs of purchasing are high, and when you come to sell you will find that estate agents' fees are generally far higher than at home. Not surprisingly, the Spanish do not buy and sell their homes as frequently as the British. I strongly recommend that you rent first to avoid making expensive and time-consuming mistakes. You can take your time getting to know your area at your leisure and, indeed, visit other areas within easy reach, before making a decision that can affect your life positively or negatively for many years to come.

In deciding where to start, it is a good idea to list the factors that are important to you. These are likely to include many of the following.

Climate

Spain is a large country, with a landscape and climate that vary greatly from one region to another. The hottest areas are undoubtedly the Costa del Sol and the Canary Islands, followed by the other Mediterranean *costas* from south to north and the Balearic Islands. On the Costa Brava you will need to heat your home in winter. Note that even in the Costa del Sol, if you live a short distance inland from the coast, you will also need heating during the winter.

The waters washing the Costa de la Luz are from the Atlantic Ocean and are much colder those of the Mediterranean. The North Atlantic coast is cooler still. Here the climate is temperate and humid. Winter weather is cold and wet and much more like the winters in the UK. Inland Spain, including Madrid, has a definitely continental climate with extremely hot summers and very cold winters. Much of inland Spain is mountainous with cold winters and cool summers. Indeed, Spain is the second most mountainous country in Europe (after Switzerland). Many areas are very arid with only occasional rainfall, and in some of these the rain can be torrential resulting in serious flooding (see below).

While geographical location is important, ensure also that the property you buy faces south – in particular its main balconies, terraces and gardens.

Property prices

There are so many different factors that determine property prices that it is unwise to overgeneralize about different regions. Much depends on a property's exact location within a region, its proximity to local facilities and communication routes, its condition and views – to mention only some of the matters that influence price. Even the condition of the neighbouring property may have a very significant effect on the price of the property for sale. It is safe to say, however, that the cheapest properties are those in rural areas, particularly the least populated, while coastal areas tend to be among the most popular and most expensive. Indeed, well over 95 per cent of foreigners purchasing property in Spain buy in coastal areas.

The following is an indication of what you might be able to purchase currently in different price ranges.

Up to 80,000 euros	a farmhouse on the Costa del Azahar in need of restoration; a variety of types of property in and around Benidorm on the Costa Blanca; a small apartment on the Costa de Almería; a house inland from the Atlantic coast in need of some restoration.
Around 100,000 euros	apartments in many older blocks in Torremolinos or Fuengirola; a small apartment on Minorca; a small apartment on Lanzarote; a two-bedroom apartment on La Gomera.
Around 120,000 euros	a villa with a sizeable garden inland on the Costa Dorado; a modest-sized house on the outskirts of Valencia; an apartment near Torrevieja on the Costa Blanca; an inland villa on the Costa de Almería in need of some restoration;

	an inland house on Majorca requiring significant repairs; a small apartment on the western side of Palma Bay on Majorca; a two-bedroom apartment, or inland rural house on Tenerife; a small apartment on Gran Canaria.
Around 200,000 euros	a villa with a sizeable garden on the Costa Dorado; a reasonably sized villa near Mazarrón and the resort of Puerto de Mazarrón on the Costa Blanca; a villa near the North Atlantic coast; an apartment on Ibiza.
Around 250,000 euros	a modest three-bedroom villa on the Costa Brava; a reasonably sized villa on the Costa de Almería; a modest-sized villa near Torrevieja, or La Manga on the Costa Blanca; a villa near the coast on the Costa de la Luz; a villa on Minorca; a reasonably sized villa on Tenerife; a modest villa on Fuerteventura.
Around 300,000 euros	a small apartment at Sotogrande on the Costa del Sol; a modest villa in parts of Gran Canaria.
Around 500,0000 euros	a villa at Sotogrande, or a modest villa near Marbella on the Costa del Sol; a reasonably good villa on Majorca.
Around 600,000 euros	a large apartment in a smart area of Barcelona; a villa on Ibiza.

Areas most popular with expatriates

The areas most favoured by the British are the Costa del Sol, the Costa Blanca, the Canary Islands and the Balearic Islands. On the Costa de Almeria the resort of Mojacar Playa is popular, on the Costa Brava there is a significant British presence to the north of Blanes, and on the Costa Tropical in the resorts of Herradura and Almunecar. There are very few British residents or property owners on the Costa Dorado, the Costa del Azahar, the Costa de la Luz and the North Atlantic coast.

Employment

How secure is your employment? If you may at some point need to obtain employment you may need to be within striking distance of one of the main cities, such as Barcelona or Valencia. Many Britons find employment in English-speaking businesses, or set up on their own providing a service to fellow English speakers, making use of contacts established within the various expatriate groups and associations.

Crime

For the most part crime is not a serious problem in Spain, save for pick-pocketing and 'lager louts' in the busiest tourist areas. Remote houses can be vulnerable. This is less true of rural village properties – a stranger will find their presence noted by the locals, and this discourages theft and break-ins.

Noise and pollution

Properties adjacent to motorways, airports and industrial areas tend to be cheaper for obvious reasons. Do not assume that life in the countryside is necessarily peaceful. Watch out for motorway and train routes – both those already constructed and those planned. Nearby church bells can shatter the quiet of a Sunday morning, not to mention the presence of a cockerel (or worse still a peacock), keen to provide a wake-up call early every morning of every week of every year, with reminders during the day. In rural Spain, it is common for many families to keep their own hens (and cockerel). Indeed, these have also been known to disturb town dwellers.

Tourists

Spain is one of the most popular European tourist destinations. Remember that some areas that are quiet in low season are overrun by tourists in the summer, and you may find yourself having to join them, on grid-locked roads that resemble overflowing car parks, stifling in the heat. On the other hand, some property owners on the Costa del Sol, for example, rent out their properties over the summer, charging rentals many times their monthly mortgage payments. This easily finances their own holidays in less hectic and less stifling holiday resorts! Equally, some parts of tourist areas have the appearance of ghost towns or villages for much of the year.

Education

If you have children of school age, you may wish to send them to a British or US school or an international school. There are several such schools, with most choice available on the Costa del Sol. There are many British and foreign children in Spanish state schools, but in some schools this is causing considerable strain on the teaching staff, concern to Spanish parents and animosities between the Spanish children and those who do not speak Spanish well.

If you wish to send your children to a private Spanish school, there are numerous Catholic schools available, but relatively few private non-Catholic schools. Further details of schools for each region are set out in Chapter 2 and Appendix 1.

Proximity of facilities

If you are elderly or suffer from bad health you should avoid remote areas and consider settling not too far from centres of medical care. On the other hand, living a little inland may enable you to rent or purchase a larger property and enjoy living without the restrictions imposed on occupants of apartment blocks. You do, however, need to bear in mind the advantages of having shops, restaurants and other facilities around the corner. There are very few retirement homes in Spain, though recent years have seen the construction of a number of retirement developments in Andalusia aimed at Europeans, and indeed the Japanese, particularly on the Costa del Sol. This is surely a field in which some enterprising ex-patriates will establish themselves in the coming years.

The local population

Inhabitants of different regions have different reputations. Generalizations are dangerous and, in any event, invariably subject to exceptions. That said, the inhabitants of Galicia and Asturias on the Northern Atlantic coast are said to be particularly welcoming and friendly. The most important ingredient in settling in any area of Spain, however, is your own determination to participate in the community into which you have moved. In Spain you have the choice of living almost entirely amongst fellow Britons, or living in a completely Spanish world, or of opting for a middle course. Whichever direction you follow, the willingness and ability to learn to speak Spanish well will stand you in good stead. It will enable you to participate in the local Spanish community if that is your wish, or at least to facilitate your dealings with the Spanish administrative authorities. Remember that in some areas, such as the Costa Brava, Costa Dorado and the Costa del Azahar, the main language is Catalan. Spanish is also the second language in much of the region bordering on the Atlantic coast.

Transport links to the UK

Even if you prefer to live in the countryside, you may wish to be within easy reach of Madrid, other major cities and the UK. The proximity of an airport with low-cost flights home and to other destinations can be important. easyJet, Ryanair, BMI Baby, Flybe, Monarch and more recently Jet 2 from Leeds/Bradford have flights to destinations throughout Spain. Malaga is particularly well served with low-cost flights to a good selection of UK airports.

I have listed most major air links with UK airports for each region in Chapter 2, although the lists are not exhaustive, with an overall list in Appendix 2.

Availability of English-speaking contacts

You may wish to socialize with other English speakers. If you do, there are numerous British and English-speaking contact organizations, especially on the Costa del Sol. The Royal British Legion and the Royal Air Force Association have various branches. There are also quite a few English-speaking churches of all denominations. The Anglican Church in particular has several churches on the *costas*. Some areas have sports clubs, women's groups, Conservative and Labour associations, Scottish associations, amateur dramatic and choral groups.

British/Irish/US goods and services

There are British, US and international schools that offer teaching in English, language schools, libraries and international bookshops at various locations in Spain. There are also numerous local English-language newspapers and magazines and several English radio stations. There are various English (and Spanish) stores selling British, US and Irish food and other products. Iceland has several branches in Spain. There are also many English (and Irish) pubs scattered throughout Spain. Not surprisingly, these are concentrated in the more popular areas. Various companies deliver British groceries and other products. These companies include Life's Little Luxuries (tel: 0190 561 1499; Web site: www.lifeslittleluxuries.co.uk), Expat Direct (tel: 0797 480 7557; Web site: www.expat-direct.co.uk) and Expat Essentials (020 8400 1527; Web site: www.expatessentials.co.uk).

Flooding

Coastal areas in parts of Spain share the same kinds of floods that have so dramatically devastated some towns in southern France. In the autumn and winter, cold air passing over the mountains inland meets the build up of hot, humid air coming from the Mediterranean. The resultant rainfall can last several days, causing severe flooding. Several areas have suffered from flood damage in the last few years. In 2001 extensive flooding caused substantial damage in Alicante and several of the coastal resorts. There was also serious flood damage more recently in December 2003, when beach properties in Guardamar Del Segura, also on the Costa Blanca, collapsed as high seas washed away foundations.

2 The regions

Mainland Spain is divided into 17 autonomous regions, with greater developed powers being granted to the traditionally more independent provinces of the Basque country, Galicia and Catalonia (which includes the Costa Brava, the Costa Dorado and the Costa del Azahar). The local regions are responsible for education, health and regional transport. In some regions, most notably the Basque country and Catalonia, there is a constant power struggle between different levels of government, which often makes dealing with administrative problems extremely difficult.

THE REGIONS OF SPAIN

THE CANARY ISLANDS

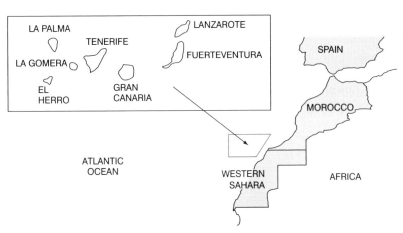

The above map shows the 17 regions of Spain. The information in this chapter, however, is set out according to the coastal areas. The names of these should mean more to many Britons familiar with Spain, and it is in these areas that the vast majority of those contemplating a move to Spain will wish to settle.

Costa Brava and northwards

Costa Brava means 'rugged coast'. Strictly applied, the term refers to that short stretch of rocky coast between Palamos and Begur east of Girona, pitted with coves that can often only be reached via steep narrow tracks. In practice, the term Costa Brava is often used to refer to the entire coast from Barcelona north-wards to the French border. This spectacular and varied coastline was one of the first to welcome the hordes of tourists from northern Europe in the late 1950s and 1960s. It has nevertheless attracted relatively few foreign residents, despite the low cost of living, and reasonably priced accommo-dation. The main significant foreign presence is in some of the resorts to the north of Blanes, which are populated especially by Britons or

Germans. Parts of the coast are increasingly becoming a commuter belt for those working in Barcelona, or a popular location for their weekend breaks.

The coastal strip from Barcelona northwards as far as Callela is very narrow as the mountains reach almost to the coast. Beyond Callela is a wider coastal plain. It is here, up towards the rocky coast from Palamos, that the main tourist resorts of the Costa Brava have been built, along the wide sandy beaches, such as those at Blanes and Platja d'Aro, or the rather less attractive but very lively Lloret de Mar. The area is highly developed and there is relatively little new construction. Property prices here are accordingly quite high. The coastline further north, beyond the 'rugged' coast and from the mouth of the river Ter, is again home to a number of resorts, including Roses.

Barcelona, a major cultural centre, is by far the largest city in the region and, with a population of 1.5 million, is Spain's second city. Like the rest of the Costa Brava, Barcelona is part of Catalonia, and Catalan is compulsory in all Spanish schools. Most of the population speaks Spanish as well as Catalan.

The area is also home to a substantial number of important archaeological sites, including the Roman ruins at Ampurias. There is a Dali museum at Figueres, the birthplace of Salvador Dali, and in 2004 there will be celebrations marking the 100th anniversary of his birth.

Water sports are particularly popular on this coast, as on most of the Spanish *costas*, and there are many marinas and sailing clubs. Scuba diving is also popular. Facilities on land include several golf courses, and the winter ski resorts in the Pyrenees are only an hour away by car. The area is rich in cultural activities and events, not merely in Barcelona, but also Cadaqués (which has an international music festival), Tossa de Mar and Blanes. The region has a number of theme parks and water parks. The best shopping facilities are in Barcelona, Girona and Blanes.

The winter climate is rather colder here than on the Costa del Sol or the Costa Blanca, and you will need to heat your home during the winter months.

Property prices on the Costa Brava are on average lower than on the Coast del Sol, for example, although there are considerable variations. Coastal properties and accommodation in golf course resorts are more expensive. A modest three-bedroom villa with a garden is attainable from about 250,000 euros. In Barcelona prices tend to be considerably higher, especially in the areas most sought after by foreigners, such as in Pedralbes to the north of the city, where a large apartment can cost 600,000 euros.

British and English-speaking contacts

There are no British or international schools on the coast, though there is one British and one US school in Barcelona, and several English schools following the Spanish curriculum in English. There is a British school in Castelldefels, and an international school in Stiges (Escaan). There are many private schools, primarily Catholic, especially in Barcelona, but in these Catalan is likely to be compulsory. There is a business school: the Barcelona Business School. There is no English-language radio station on the Costa Brava, but there is a local free monthly paper entitled *Barcelona Metropolitan*. The paper has an informative Web site (www.barcelona-metropolitan.com) which has a useful section on moving to Barcelona, and details of English-language clubs, societies and associations (see under Listings and also under Useful contacts). The paper contains advertisements from a number of businesses run by Britons and other English speakers. There is also an online English-language newspaper *Cap Creus on line* (www.cbrava.com) with much information on the northern Costa Brava.

The UK, Ireland, Australia, New Zealand, Canada and the United States all have consulates in Barcelona. There are few church services in English in this region, though there is an Anglican church in Barcelona, where there is also a Catholic Church with services in English and The International (inter-denominational) Church of Barcelona. The British and English-speaking clubs and associations are almost entirely in Barcelona, and include the Rotary Club, Alcoholics Anonymous, football clubs, a Gaelic football club, an Irish Catalan Association, the American Society, the Royal British Legion, Scottish country dancing, Conservatives Abroad, and Democrats Abroad.

The only regular showings of films in English are in Barcelona. Many of the larger supermarkets, including in the smaller resorts, have a reasonable selection of British foods. The resorts, including in particular Lloret de Mar and Tossa de Mar, have a good selection of British pubs. There are two English bookshops in Barcelona, and also a lending library operated by the British Council. There is a Hard Rock Café in Barcelona, and a warm welcome at Flaherty's Irish pub.

UK and Ireland travel links

The main airport on the Costa Brava is at Barcelona. There is also an airport at Girona, and airports in Montpelier and Perpignan over the border in France. The main routes for scheduled flights are as follows.

Barcelona: Birmingham, Bournemouth, Bristol, Dublin, East Midlands, Glasgow, Leeds/Bradford, Liverpool, London Heathrow, London Luton, London Stansted, Manchester, Newcastle

Girona: London Stansted

Montpelier: London Stansted

Perpignan: London Stansted

Other travel information

Ryanair has recently announced its intention to intensify its use of Girona airport from 2004, with proposed destinations including Paris, Rome, Venice and Stockholm, and a new bus line has been announced linking the airport with Figueres, Castello d'Empuries and Roses. There are daily ferry services from Barcelona to the Balearic Islands and a weekly service to Genoa in Italy. Blanes is 30 minutes by train from Barcelona. A high-speed train link to Madrid is due to open in 2004. There is a good motorway link from Barcelona to the French border.

Costa Dorado

The 'golden coast' stretches 300 kilometres to the south west from Barcelona, to the wetlands of the Ebro Delta. As its name suggests, this coastline boasts golden beaches that seem to extend into the horizon. Despite its superb beaches, warm climate, low cost of living and cheap property prices the region does not have many foreign property owners. That said, the northern half of the coast has a number of resorts popular with foreign holidaymakers, and as weekend locations for residents of Barcelona, most notably Stiges, only 40 minutes from Barcelona.

To the south of Stiges there are several resorts, for the most part fairly peaceful, such as those at Calafell (with its medieval castle), Comarruga, and Altafulla. Torredembarra and Tarragona are rather busier, the latter being well worth a visit to see its Roman remains and medieval buildings, including the city's cathedral. The most substantial tourist centre by far is that at Salou. It has most, if not all, of the features of a Spanish package resort, albeit a little toned down from the excesses of the most popular locations on the Costa del Sol. The resort boasts a noisy nightlife, as is true to a lesser extent of Stiges and Port Ginesta (see below). Not far from Salou is the huge theme park and resort of Universal Mediterrania.

To the south west of Salou there are a number of small coastal resorts, but access to the beaches is hampered to an extent by the railway line and the N-340 that run along the coast. These have clearly hampered the development of this section of the coast, save around the large busy resort of Miami Playa where there is substantial construction underway.

This is Catalonia and accordingly you will hear Catalan spoken almost everywhere, although there are many Spanish speakers living here, and most Catalans are bilingual. Catalan is compulsory in Spanish schools in this area.

The Costa Dorado has the full range of water sports available and boasts several marinas. Port Ginesta at Castelldefels was constructed specifically for the 1992 Olympics and has excellent facilities for an extensive range of water sports. There are several golf courses on this *costa*, which also has a number of cultural centres including at Stiges and Calafell. For shopping facilities Barcelona is excellent, but further south Reus and Tarragona have substantial shopping centres, as does Torredembarra.

Property prices are much lower than on the more popular *costas*. Prices of a villa with a sizeable garden start from about 200,000 euros, but inland you may find properties for half that price.

British and English-speaking contacts

Apart from in Barcelona, the only international school is the Anglo-American school at Castelldefels. In the Spanish private schools your child will undergo a Catholic education, and is likely to have to learn Catalan. The numbers of English speakers on the Costa Dorado do not appear sufficient to support any English-language papers, or indeed any churches, Anglican or otherwise. In Barcelona the picture is a little different with a number of churches holding services in English, including St. George's Anglican Church. In Barcelona there is also a monthly publication in English (*Barcelona Metropolitan* – see above under Costa Brava) and several cinemas showing English-language films in their original version. The larger supermarkets stock various British food items, and at the larger resorts you will find a selection of British and Irish pubs.

UK and Ireland travel links

The main airport serving the Costa Dorado is that at Barcelona, though there is also an airport at Reus. The main routes for scheduled flights are as follows.

Barcelona: Birmingham, Bournemouth, Bristol, Dublin, East Midlands, Glasgow, Leeds/Bradford, Liverpool, London Heathrow, London Luton, London Stansted, Manchester, Newcastle

Falcon Holidays is to start package holidays from City of Derry airport in Northern Ireland to the Costa Dorado in 2004.

Other travel information

There are ferry services to the Balearic Islands and to Genoa in Italy. There is a railway line from Barcelona to Valencia along the coast, with trains stopping at various locations including Miami Playa, Salou, Tarragona, Torredembarra and Stiges. There is also a motorway along the coast (the A-7, and to the north the A-16).

Costa del Azahar

COSTA DEL AZAHAR

This term, meaning 'orange blossom coast', refers to the coastal areas of the provinces of Valencia and Castellon. The Costa del Azahar has long sandy beaches, but despite this only a few Britons have settled here. The Germans are present, but in smaller numbers than on the other coasts. For the most part, however, the properties here belong to Spaniards, mostly from Valencia, Spain's third largest city with a population of around 750,000, the inhabitants of which flock to this coast during August.

The Albufera, a freshwater lagoon, lies to the south of Valencia, and at its southern edge you will find the resort of Cullera, the most prosperous resort to the south of Valencia. It is the northern section of this coast, however, that attracts most visitors, especially around the towns of Vinaros, Benicarlo and Peniscola, and the resort of Benicassim. Property prices are not particularly cheap, but inland there are farms in need of restoration that can be purchased at low prices, and on the outskirts of Valencia modest-sized houses start from under 100,000 euros.

Valencia has undergone a facelift in recent years and is a popular all-year congress centre, with many leisure facilities, and a wide range of cultural events. It is to host the America's Cup in 2007. Here, and throughout much of the region, the language is Valenciano, a variant of Catalan, though most people also speak Spanish.

British and English-speaking contacts

There are very few facilities catering for English speakers, except that in Valencia there are several British and international schools, as well as a selection of private Spanish schools offering a Catholic education. There are also two cinemas where English films are shown. There is no Anglican church in the region, and indeed no other church with services in English. For British and foreign food you will have to visit the El Corte Inglés, but the range is limited.

UK travel links

Valencia (Manises): London Heathrow

Other travel information

Valencia is to host the America's Cup 2007, and accordingly the airport is to undergo major expansion, including the extension of the runway and two new terminal buildings. There are scheduled but infrequent flights from Valencia to several European cities, as well as domestic services to

Madrid and Barcelona. There are motorway and rail links to Madrid and Barcelona, with a high-speed train link to Madrid under construction. Ferry services operate to the Balearic Islands.

Costa Blanca

For nearly 40 years the Costa Blanca or 'white coast', has been a favourite holiday destination for British tourists, and is second only to the Costa del Sol as a popular choice for expatriates to settle. There are now several complexes dominated by British residents. The earliest complexes to be populated by Britons were those in Javea and Altea, and more recently this has happened in Gandia in the north and La Manga in the south. This coast has an extensive network of businesses operated by English speakers.

Property prices are lower here than on the Costa del Sol, as is the cost of living. Winters here are extremely mild, and the summers are hot. The region is subject to frequent droughts as rain is in short supply, save in the autumn when the region is often subjected to extremely heavy rainfall. In 2001 this resulted in extensive flooding that caused substantial damage in Alicante and several of the coastal resorts. There was also serious flood damage more recently in December 2003, when beach properties in Guardamar Del Segura collapsed as high seas washed away foundations

The northern stretch of the Costa Blanca is the more rugged, with many picturesque and peaceful rocky coves. Inland there are high mountains such as the Montgo behind Denia, and orchards of fruit trees and vineyards lining the valleys. The main population centres are at Denia (which has many amenities, including a marina); Javea (a seaport with ancient narrow streets); Calpe (an interesting and lively town with a new marina) and Altea (unspoilt and known for its nearby scenery). There are also resorts at Moraira and further north at Gandia, and increasingly new developments are appearing slightly inland in the Jalon Valley. The most well known resort on the Costa Blanca is, of course, Benidorm, to the south of Altea, with its teeming nightlife of clubbing, cabarets, discotheques and open-air concerts. Despite its enduring popularity, property is cheaper here, thanks in part to continual construction. Progressing further south there is the slightly calmer resort of Vilajoyosa, which also benefits from the proximity of the huge newly built theme park near Terra Mitica. The Costa Blanca also has several water parks. Benidorm Sea Life Park (Mundomar) operates a dolphin therapy programme for disabled children.

The region's capital, about half-way along the Costa Blanca, is Alicante. Few tourists spend long here, and there are not many foreign residents. It has a good range of facilities, and plenty of nightlife – especially around El Barrio, the old quarter – along with the disadvantages of a large city, particularly traffic congestion and pollution.

To the south of Alicante the terrain is flatter and much more arid. The rocky coves of further north give way to long golden sandy beaches. This stretch of the Costa Blanca has only started to undergo development during the last decade, but is expanding rapidly. A considerable number of residential complexes have been constructed, of varying standards, including to the south of Torrevieja. There is a good supply of low and moderately priced properties, thanks to the high level of continuing construction. Torrevieja is a major resort with good amenities and is growing at a pace, its population doubling over the last decade, with many Britons amongst the newcomers. The town is said to be especially beneficial for those with respiratory difficulties or suffering from allergies, owing to the two salt lakes that, together with the sea, surround the resort. It has excellent leisure facilities, including a theatre and casino, and a thriving night scene. Further south is the Mar Menor, one of the most popular resorts in Spain, including during the winter months. It is a huge saltwater lagoon protected from the sea by La Manga (meaning 'sleeve') – a narrow strip of land little more than 2 kilometres at its widest point and boasting fine sandy beaches, that runs parallel to the coast. There are many sporting facilities here, especially for water sports, but including several excellent golf courses. Cycling is popular thanks to the flat terrain. This stretch of the coast has undergone substantial development in recent years, though there are no hospitals here: you will need to travel to Cartagena or Murcia (the latter being some distance away).

The Costa Calida (the 'hot coast') refers to the stretch of coastline between the Costa Blanca and the Costa Almeria to the south. It is rather undeveloped until one reaches Mazarron, and the resort of Puerto de

Mazarrón. Here you will find excellent beaches. Some information on the Costa Calida can be found on www.elojoespanol.com

The language spoken on the Costa Blanca is Valenciano, a form of Catalan, which is particularly strong towards Valencia to the north, and in the rural areas. The language is keenly supported by the local authorities, though most people also speak Spanish.

Besides the abundant sporting and leisure opportunities, especially water sports, hang-gliding and golf, on the cultural side there are several music festivals, and many local traditional festivals often accompanied by extravagant firework displays. Most of the facilities, and the vibrant nightlife here, are available all year round. There are also plenty of shopping centres in the main towns most notably in Alicante, Valencia and Benidorm, as well as a number of hypermarkets, and reasonable facilities serving the main resorts. Carrefour have recently opened a hypermarket in Vinaroz.

Property prices have increased quite significantly over the past decade, though they have not reached the levels common on the Costa del Sol. There is a wide range of different types of property available. Prices are lower on the southern stretch of the coast, and in Benidorm where you can find properties for under 80,000 euros, the cheapest being the older apartments built in the early days of the explosion of tourism. A modest-sized villa near Torrevieja, or indeed in La Manga, can cost as little as 230,000 euros, with a two-bedroom apartment costing about half that amount. Further south near Mazarrón and the resort of Puerto de Mazarrón, you will find reasonably sized villas for about 180,000 euros. The most expensive properties are in the areas favoured by the British house buyers, notably the north eastern tip of the coast between Moraira and Javea. Long-term rental property is in very short supply along the Costa Blanca.

British and English-speaking contacts

The Costa Blanca has a substantial number of British and international schools, including at Valencia and Alicante, with British schools in Javea (2), Alfas del Pi, Benidorm, and Murcia (2) , and US schools in Torrevieja and La Manga. Caxton College in Valencia, and Shoreless Lake School in Murcia have boarding facilities. There are private (Catholic) Spanish schools in most of the larger cities, including Valencia, Alicante and Benidorm. There are a substantial number of Anglican churches in the region (including at Alicante, Alcocebre, Calpe, Campello, Denia, Gandia, Jávea, La Manga, La Marina, Teulada/Moraira, Benidorm, Orba/Orbeta, La Siesta, Lago Jardin, Los Balcónes and Torrevieja), and also Baptist and Evangelical (both in Jávea) and Catholic services in English (including at Benidorm).

A considerable number of English-language publications can be found on the Costa Blanca, most notably *Costa Blanca News* (its Web site at www.costablanca-news.com includes a list of English-speaking businesses), *Valencia Life, Views Magazine, The Weekly Post, The Euro Weekly News* and, in Benidorm, *Look What's On*. There is also an English-language radio station Onda Cero International (94.6 FM) broadcasting full time in English. The Costa Blanca has an extensive range of clubs and associations run by English speakers. These cover sports, theatre (including in Denia, Orba and Jávea) and politics, as well as social groups and also charitable organizations, a Classic Cars club, a yoga group and a Gilbert and Sullivan society. There are a number of cinemas on the coast showing English-language films, including at Calpe, Gata, Jávea Port and Benidorm. Save in Alicante, most supermarkets sell a range of British food products, though prices are often high. There are many British pubs and restaurants, especially in Benidorm and the other main resorts.

Information about English-speaking services on the Costa Blanca is available on www.costablancasearch.com. This information includes services in Alicante, Jávea, Torrevieja, Jalón, Altea, Campello, Benidorm, Calpe, Denia and La Marina.

The UK, Denmark, the Netherlands, Norway and Sweden have consulates in Alicante. The Netherlands and Sweden also have consulates in Benidorm.

UK and Ireland travel links

The Costa Blanca is served by three airports. Chief among them is El Altet, outside Alicante, providing many flights to the UK and other European destinations. The airport of Manises, close to the city of Valencia, and San Javier Murcia airport, serving the southern half of the Costa Blanca, also have flights to the UK, in the latter case charter flights. The main routes for scheduled flights are as follows.

Alicante:	Bristol, Dublin, East Midlands, Leeds/Bradford, Liverpool, London Gatwick, London Luton, London Stansted, Manchester, Newcastle
Murcia:	Birmingham, East Midlands, Leeds/Bradford, London Gatwick, London Stansted
Valencia:	London Heathrow

Other travel information

All three airports handle domestic flights, in particular to Madrid and Barcelona. There are regular ferry services from Alicante and Denia to the Balearic Islands, and from Alicante to Oran in Algeria. Unlike many regions of Spain, the Costa Blanca has a developed road network, though the N 332 in particular is subject to severe congestion, especially where it passes through the coastal resorts, and improvements are planned. Public transport is reasonably good. A new bus link has recently opened between Alicante airport and Benidorm. There are rail links from Madrid to Alicante, and a good train service from Denia to Alicante with several stops including at Calpe. In late 2003 new plans were announced for a high-speed train link from Alicante to Murcia.

Costa de Almería

The coastline to either side of the town of Almería is completely unspoilt, but includes a number of popular resorts. To the south is Aquadulce with its marina, and the more modern and busier complexes at Roquetas del Mar, Playa Serena and Almerimar, with a number of marinas and golf courses. To the north of Almería is the rugged and desolate coast of the Cabo del Gato-Nijar natural park, and further north the expanding resorts of Mojacar Playa and Vera, the latter boasting a number of naturist beaches.

This region of Spain is one of the hottest, sunniest and most arid. Average winter temperatures seldom fall below 15 C. Inland, much of the terrain consists of desert, the scene for the filming of many a western, with a Hollywood-type theme park at Tabernas. Large parts of this desert terrain have proved extremely fertile when watered, and there are now seemingly endless expanses of the region covered in plastic-sheeted greenhouses under which much of northern Europe's supply of winter vegetables are grown. This has resulted in an additional huge source of new wealth for this very prosperous region.

The population of this area has grown considerably in recent years, in large part due to the arrival of substantial numbers of economic migrants from Eastern Europe and North Africa, working in the expanding agricultural sector. To date, the only resort to see substantial numbers of foreigners is that of Mojacar Playa, where a high proportion of residents are British.

There is an extensive array of water sports available on the Costa de Almería, with scuba diving and sailing being particularly popular. Almeria has a good range of shops, but elsewhere choices are more limited especially out of season. Dining out is generally rather more expensive than on the Costa del Sol.

Property prices are lower than on the Costa del Sol and properties are in good supply owing to the extent of new construction that is taking place. Two-bedroom apartments start at about 75,000 euros, and villas at about 200,000 euros. Inland you may be able to find houses for about half that amount, though they will probably need significant work carried out.

The area is presently undergoing considerable development in order to participate in the hosting of the Mediterranean Games in 2005.

British and English-speaking contacts

There are no British or international schools on the Costa de Almería. It appears, however, that a new international school is to open in 2005 (probably near Turre) catering for children aged from 5 to 12 and offering a bilingual education with a curriculum based upon the International Baccalaureate. Enquiries should be sent to intschoolsespain@cs.com. A new nursery is also due to open this year (2004) in Antas. There are, of course, several private (mainly Catholic) Spanish schools in the region. The small numbers of English speakers here do not warrant any English-language publication, but you may find the Costa del Sol publications worth looking at. British food products are available in some of the larger supermarkets, but are expensive.

There are Anglican services at Mojacar, Los Castanos, Aguilas, Costacabana and El Agua de Enmediot, Roman Catholic services at Mojacar Village Church and an Evangelical church at Cuevas. There are several local clubs and societies including bowling, Alcoholics Anonymous, amateur radio, cricket, gardening, archery, theatre, tennis, branches of the Royal British Legion and Weight Watchers.

Information in English, including details of English-speaking contacts and services, is available on the Web site www.elojoespanol.com, which covers in particular Vera, Garrucha, Mojacar, and Carboneras, and also the Costa Calida, and has a number of chat pages. The Web site www.andalucia.com is also worth inspecting, as it has a section on the Costa de Almeria.

UK and Ireland travel links

The largest airport serving the region is that at Alicante, with flights to nine UK destinations and also to Dublin. Almeria is smaller, but with services to several UK destinations. Murcia airport also has an increasing number of flights to the UK. The main routes for scheduled flights are as follows.

Alicante:	Bristol, Dublin, East Midlands, Leeds/Bradford, Liverpool, London Gatwick, London Luton, London Stansted, Manchester, Newcastle
Almería:	London Gatwick
Murcia:	Birmingham, East Midlands, Leeds/Bradford, London Gatwick, London Stansted

Other travel information

You will definitely need a car. Bus and train services leave a great deal to be desired. The road network has recently started to undergo long-needed improvements, and Almería is to have 200 kilometres of new roads and two new highways by 2010. This should go some considerable way towards reducing the region's remoteness, and perhaps improve the rather slow-moving route to the Costa del Sol.

Costa Tropical and the Alpujarras

COSTA TROPICAL

The most northern stretch of the Costa del Sol, known as the Costa Tropical, is quiet and undeveloped. In truth, there is very little space in which to construct, as the mountains of the Sierra Nevada come down very close to the coastline, and in places into the sea. There are a number of small villages along the coast, but only two substantial resorts, those of La Herradura and Almuñécar. Salobrena is also popular, a whitewashed town topping an outcrop of rock just back from the shoreline, and boasting a Moorish 10th-century castle. There are a number of villas dotted around the hillsides. To the east of Motril, where the beaches are wider, a number of developments have recently been constructed.

Property prices on the Costa Tropical are low, and you will have no difficulty finding a house under 100,000 euros, although prices are considerably higher in Herradura and Almuñécar. There is an international school in Almuñécar in which the UK National Curriculum is taught and pupils take GCSE and A level examinations.

Inland from the coast are Las Alpujarras, on the lower reaches of the Sierra Nevada. This area is known for its stunning views and tranquillity, and is a popular visiting place for Spaniards seeking some time 'away from it all'. The views here are truly spectacular, but this is very much an isolated and undeveloped part of Spain (the nearest airports are those of Almería and Malaga), with a fiercely cold climate in winter with many routes becoming impassable in wet weather. The town of Trevélez, for example, is said to be the highest village in Europe. The area is only sparsely populated, with the largest town in the region, Berja, having a population under 15,000. The area's administrative capital Orgiva has a mere 5,000 inhabitants.

There are few facilities in Las Alpujarras, though green tourism is rapidly increasing in popularity, and there is of course skiing in the Sierra Nevada further inland. There are very few foreigners living in the area, and accordingly few services catering for them, apart from the international school in Almuñécar. Public transport is poor or non-existent.

Useful information about the Costa Tropical is available on www.andalucia.com with details concerning Almuñécar, and Salobrena. For travel information see below under Costa del Sol.

Costa del Sol

COSTA DEL SOL

The Costa del Sol, on the south coast of Spain in Andalusia, is by far the most popular area for British property buyers, with more choosing to buy here than in the whole of the rest of Spain. There are almost 3 million homes here owned by foreigners, with estimates of the number of Britons resident ranging up to 500,000, with well over 200,000 Germans also choosing to settle here. The Costa del Sol stretches from nearly as far south as Gibraltar, towards Matril in the north, and is dominated by the tourist industry, with 9 million visitors a year. The region's capital is Malaga, Spain's fifth largest city, with a population of around 500,000. While much of the coast has an international feel, Malaga is neither a major tourist attraction nor a popular choice with foreign residents. It has retained its Spanish character and its Arab past – the city was under Muslim rule until the latter years of the 15th century.

The Costa del Sol is an ideal choice for the foreign property buyer. It boasts excellent weather, with over 320 days of sun each year and mild winters (average January temperatures are about 16°C). It is easily accessible via the airport at Malaga. It has an extensive range of sports and leisure activities (most notably golf and water sports, but also skiing in the Sierra Nevada, some two hours from the coast by car). In many areas foreigners make up a substantial proportion of the population, with the British being the most numerous, followed by the Germans and then the Scandinavians. Not surprisingly, in summer the beaches are crammed, and in places traffic is almost at a standstill.

There has been extensive construction of hotels, apartment blocks and a host of different types of housing developments (*urbanizaciones*) over the last 40 years. The region continues to expand – its population is expected to increase by a further 50 per cent over the next decade. The improvement of the road network and other infrastructure has tended to lag behind, and is likely to continue to do so. The region has a considerable number of marinas, theme and water parks and a safari park.

South of Estepona, however, there has been far less construction than elsewhere on the Costa del Sol, save at Sotogrande (about an hour from Malaga airport along the A-7 motorway) where there is a purpose-built luxury development, and many upmarket properties. It is this stretch of the coast, down towards Gibraltar, that is known as the Costa del Golf, and is home to a good number of dedicated golf resorts, especially around Sotogrande. The Valderrama Golf Club at Sotogrande is the site of a world championship course. Estepona and San Pedro de Alcantara are expanding, and both have a significant British presence. Inland is the Serrania de Ronda, a series of valleys with very attractive villages and where many foreigners have built or purchased substantial properties in which to enjoy the tranquillity of the mountains.

The most popular and expensive location is undoubtedly Marbella with its famous marina of Puerto Banus, the new town of Nueva Andalucia and 'Golf Valley' close by. Further up the coast is Mijas Costa and the busy town of Fuengirola. In Mijas itself it is estimated that well over 40 per cent of the occupants are foreign. In between here and Malaga are the resort of Banalmádena and the package holiday resort of Torremolinos, the latter being one of the first sites to be developed in the early days of mass tourism, with its noisy nightlife, high-rise blocks and its plentiful supply of a rather unhealthy variety of British cuisine. Benalmádena is newer than Torremolinos, but expanding rapidly with a substantial number of British residents and a good range of facilities. As one passes Malaga, progressing north-east along the coast, the region again becomes far less developed, and more tranquil, though the coastal resorts are still crowded during the summer months. Nerja, famous for its caves, is particularly popular with the British, and has a fairly good range of leisure and cultural activities. There are several small- to medium-sized resorts along this stretch of the coast, including Cala de Moral, and Torre del Mar. Inland from Torre del Mar the scenery is quite spectacular.

The cost of property on the Costa del Sol is substantially higher than in the rest of Spain, especially in and around Marbella, and has increased substantially in the last few years. The coast is undergoing rapid development, with new residential complexes constantly under construction.

VIVA Estates

For five years VIVA Estates has realised the dreams of thousands of eager home hunters wishing to enjoy an improved quality of life under the Spanish sun. Through constant innovation, consistently excellent levels of customer service and an unceasing commitment to finding the perfect property for every customer, VIVA has become the leading real estate specialist on the Costa del Sol.

Now with ten area offices stretching from Torremolinos to Sotogrande, VIVA is ideally placed to handle all requirements and answer all questions involved in home hunting abroad. VIVA's 220 property experts are able to provide comprehensive information not just on the complete buying process but also on living and working on the coast, covering everything from education and healthcare to lifestyle and relocation advice.

Offering the complete property purchasing solution, VIVA's impressive range of services ensures a smooth path to house-buying in Spain. Home hunters can search through a host of new developments and over 4000 re-sale properties in addition to seeking independent financial advice from VIVA's partner, Green Independent and gaining access to respected Marbella lawyers. The service doesn't end with the purchase either, since VIVA's Homecare department are then available to provide furnishing, maintenance and decorating assistance along with regular updates on projects awaiting completion. For customers wishing to generate income from property abroad VIVA recently launched its lettings departments, whilst home-owners looking to sell their property can benefit from coverage in VIVA's extensive marketing programme.

VIVA boasts unrivalled knowledge of the Costa del Sol, the first choice destination for British residents looking to realise their dream of a place in the sun. The sun shines for an average of 325 days a year and winter temperatures resemble those similar to a British summer. Only a 2½ hour flight from the UK, the coast is a million miles from the rat race, and despite a booming economy Spain is still famed for its relaxed and laidback lifestyle.

With all this in mind it's no surprise that thousands of people have chosen VIVA Estates as their partner on the path to a new lifestyle on the sunshine coast.

The speed with which new accommodation is being built invariably exceeds the creation of the infrastructure required, and in many cases it is some years before important services such as a public transport network, medical facilities and schools are put in place. The cheaper properties (priced at well under 100,000 euros) include many apartments in the older blocks in the busier resorts, such as Torremolinos or Fuengirola, although the standard of these properties is not as high as in the more recent developments. In Sotogrande, on the other hand, apartments start at over 300,000 and villas from 450,000. Marbella tends to be a little dearer still, though both Mijas and Nerja are rather less expensive (especially the latter). Inland, property prices tend to be lower, but there are few amenities, the roads and other infrastructure are poor, and few foreigners choose to settle or buy there. Long-term rentals are difficult to find on the Costa del Sol, though there is an ample supply of properties for short-term letting.

In addition to the many sporting opportunities available on the Costa del Sol, the region has several theme and water parks and a large safari park near Estepona. The region is also home to an extensive range of cultural activities, including annual film festivals in Marbella and Malaga. There is a wide range of shops.

The medical facilities on the Costa del Sol are generally good, with the public hospital in Marbella, and the children's hospital El Materno, in particular having a reputation for a high standard of care. Marbella boasts a number of private clinics, including some specializing in cosmetic surgery and claiming to be leaders in this field. There are several British qualified doctors and dentists practising on the Costa del Sol. Recent years have seen the first retirement homes opening on the coast, a new development in Spain.

Useful information about the Costa del Sol is available at www.andalucia.com

British and English-speaking contacts

There are many English-language speakers established on the Costa del Sol, running an extensive range of different businesses serving the English-speaking community.

There is a university in Malaga with a plentiful supply of courses in Spanish, and the area contains a good number of British and international co-educational schools, especially in and around Marbella (for a detailed list see www.andalucia.com education – schools, and also the Web site of the National Association of British Schools in Spain (www.nabss.org). The majority of these schools follow the UK curriculum (with National Curriculum tests, GCSE and A levels), although some programmes of study are based on the International Baccalaureate. The English International School (tel: 952 83 10 58) in Marbella, founded in 1982, provides education for children aged from 3 to 18, and claims to have the best results of the British schools in Spain. The Swans International Primary School (tel: 952 77 32 48) puts an emphasis on learning foreign languages, and in addition to teaching Spanish has a French national teacher to teach French. Other schools include Aloha College (tel: 952 81 41 33) also in Marbella where the curriculum at sixth form follows the International Baccalaureate, Sunny View School (tel: 952 38 31 64) in Torremolinos, The International School at Sotogrande (tel: 956 79 59 02) and St Anthony's College in Mijas (tel: 952 24 73 16). There are also French, German, Norwegian and Swedish schools on the Costa del Sol. There are a number of private Spanish schools. Of particular note is San José College (tel: 952 88 38 58), popular with many foreign residents in Marbella, whose children make up a large proportion of the pupils at the school.

In some areas there are substantial numbers of British children in Spanish state schools, placing a great strain on the ability of these schools to cope with the numbers of non-Spanish speakers. In one school in Mijas, about half the children are foreign, mainly British, and only 4 per cent of these speak Spanish well. Some Spanish parents are naturally concerned that their children's education is suffering, as the teachers have to spend a disproportionate amount of their time helping the foreign pupils. In some schools there is intense rivalry and hostility between the local Spanish children and the English-speaking children.

The region has a large number of churches of all denominations catering for English-speaking residents. There are Anglican/Episcopalian churches or services in Malaga, Nerja, Torre del Mar, Almuñécar, Los Boliches, Competa, Fuengirola, Benalmádena Costa, Calahonda, Coin, San Pedro/Estepona, Sotogrande, Gaucin, Torremolinos and Gibraltar. There are Roman Catholic masses in English at churches in Marbella, Arroyo de la Miel, Calahonda, Los Boliches and Benalmádena Costa, Presbyterian services in Fuengirola and Gibraltar, Methodist congregations in Gibraltar and Sotogrande, and Evangelical or Baptist services in a number of locations including Torremolinos, Fuengirola, Marbella, Motril and Gibraltar. There is a synagogue in Torremolinos and mosques in Marbella, Fuengirola and Malaga. Further details, including contact names and telephone numbers, can be found on the *Sur in English* Web site: www.surinenglish.com under 'church'. If you intend to join any of these congregations it is worthwhile making contact before you leave, as the minister and the members of the congregation are likely to have much local knowledge that they will be willing to pass on if asked.

There are regular showings of films in English at Puerto Banus. There are branches of Bookworld in San Pedro and Fuengirola (tel: 952 66 48 37), a card shop at Benavista (Rita's), and a second hand bookshop in San Pedro de Alcantara (Shakespeare), just off the N-340 between Estepona and Marbella. British food can be purchased at most of the region's supermarkets, including at Iceland, and at more specialist British food shops. There are several branches of the Irish store Dunnes in the region and further south in Gibraltar branches of Safeway and British Home Stores. The wide range of Britons and other native English speakers in business on the Costa del Sol includes doctors and lawyers, architects and estate agents.

The English-language press is an invaluable source of information, and includes *Sur in English* (Web site: www.surinenglish.com), *Costa del Sol News, Essential Marbella, Absolute Marbella, Andalucia Golf Magazine* and *The Reporter.* There are several English-language radio stations broadcasting on the Costa del Sol, including Onda Cero International, Coastline Radio and Global Radio.

There is a vast range of clubs and associations run by and for native English speakers. These include the Royal British Legion (eight branches across the region), the Royal Air Forces Association, The American Club (seven branches across the region), the Rotary Club, the Lions Club, Alcoholics Anonymous, Conservatives Abroad, Democrats Abroad, and a Labour Group. There are also associations for line dancing, music, amateur theatre, yoga, barbershop singers, surfing, flower arranging, skiing, gardening, and even an Achievers Toastmasters Club meeting in Puerto Banus.

British and foreign food is widely available. There are many English and Irish pubs, especially in the main centres, such as O'Grady's Irish Tavern in Puerto Banus (a somewhat noisy establishment with its big screen and karaoke evenings), and the American Corner (a 1960s bar), also in Puerto Banus. Gibraltar has several British chain stores and other outlets selling products popular in the UK.

The UK, Canada, the Netherlands and Norway have consulates in Malaga, and Ireland and Sweden have consulates in Fuengirola.

UK and Ireland travel links

Malaga: Bristol, Dublin, East Midlands, Leeds/Bradford, Liverpool, London Gatwick, London Heathrow, London Luton, London Stansted, Manchester

Gibraltar: London Gatwick, London Heathrow, Luton, Manchester

Other travel information

Public transport is limited. There is a train service from Malaga to Torremolinos, Benalmadena and Fuengirola. A new railway line is soon to be constructed from Malaga to Nerja. There are bus links from the airport to Malaga and Marbella; and ferry links from Malaga to Melilla, the Spanish enclave on the Moroccan coast, and the Balearic Islands. The train journey to Madrid currently takes about four hours, but in 2004 should be reduced to well under three hours thanks to the introduction of a new high-speed train. The A-7 toll motorway, the Autopista del Sol that runs along the coast, provides a good alternative to the busy N-340.

Costa de la Luz

COSTA
DE LA LUZ

The 'coast of light' is the Atlantic section of Spain's southern coast, stretching from the southern-most tip of Andalusia at Punta Tarifa (about 20 kilometres west of Gibraltar) to the Portuguese border. Here the sea is much colder than along the Mediterranean coastline, the currents and the winds much stronger. Despite its warm sunny climate, miles of stunning beaches and splendid sand dunes, and relatively low property prices, the Costa de la Luz has been far less popular than most of the other *costas*, and the area is only just beginning to be developed.

The Costa de la Luz is split in half by the Doñana National Park, a huge nature reserve in the marshes at the mouth of the river Guadalquivir, boasting many wild animals including cattle, deer and eagles. Entry into the park is restricted, and to drive from the port of Cadiz towards Huelva and the border with Portugal to the west requires a long detour via Seville to the north. To the west of Doñana there is a substantial development at Matalascañas with hotels, villa complexes and golf courses. Further west towards the Portuguese border, there are a number of smaller developments interspersed between the few coastal villages. Playa de Mazagón, Playa de la Antilla and Fuenebravia are popular. Inland from Cadiz is Jerez de la Frontera, famous for its sherry, and its riding school.

The coast south of Cadiz has a number of resorts, including the increasingly popular Novo Sancti Petri near Chiclana, and the rapidly developing complex of Zahara de los Atunes, between Barbate and Tarifa. In the last 20 years the fishing port of Tarifa has been transformed following its discovery as one of the best windsurfing locations in Europe, if not the best.

Apart from water sports, the region has far fewer amenities than the more popular *costas*. There are a good number of golf courses, however, and a Formula 1 racecourse at Jerez. During the winter the resorts here, in contrast to those on the Costa del Sol, tend to be almost deserted. There is a huge difference between spending time here in the summer months and during the rest of the year. As one would expect, Algeciras, Cadiz and Jerez all have good shopping centres, but elsewhere the facilities are more limited, especially during the winter months. There is a good selection of shops in Gibraltar. The historic city of Seville, with a population of 700,000, is not far away and is well worth a visit. It has excellent shopping facilities, but suffers from traffic pollution, congestion and noise, and stifling temperatures averaging 35°C during July and August.

Property prices on the Costa de la Luz are much lower than on the Costa del Sol. Prices vary, but you will find three bedroom villas available from about 250,000 euros, with prices lower inland, especially for properties in near of repair.

British and English-speaking contacts

There are no British or US schools on the Costa de la Luz, or in Seville, though there is a bilingual international school in Jerez following a Spanish curriculum, and another international school further up the coast in

Sotogrande. The larger towns have private schools, most of which offer a Catholic education. There are insufficient numbers of English speakers here to warrant an English-language radio station or newspaper. Similarly there are no English-language church services, nor many films shown in English.

The UK, the United States and Australia all have consulates in Seville. Useful information about the region can be found on the Web site www.andalucia.com

UK and Ireland travel links

There are airports at Jerez and Seville, but for the most parts flights are only internal. Most foreigners arrive via Malaga airport, with some, mainly from British airports, arriving through Gibraltar. Resorts to the west are better accessed via Faro airport in Portugal. The main routes for scheduled flights from the UK and Ireland are as follows.

Jerez de la Frontera: London Stansted

Malaga: Bristol, Dublin, East Midlands, Leeds/Bradford, Liverpool, London Gatwick, London Heathrow, London Luton, London Stansted, Manchester

Gibraltar: London Gatwick, London Heathrow, Luton, Manchester

Faro: Bristol, Dublin, Leeds/Bradford, East Midlands, London Luton, London Stansted, Manchester

Seville: London Gatwick

Other travel information

There are ferry routes from Cadiz to the Canary Islands, from Algeciras to Ceuta, the Spanish-ruled city in Morocco, and from Gibraltar to Tangiers.

The North Atlantic coast

NORTH ATLANTIC COAST

The North Atlantic coast, cut off from central Spain by the Cantabrian mountains, consists of the four regions of Galicia in the far north-west, Asturias, Cantabria, and the Basque country on the border with France. The region boasts some of the most stunning beaches in the Iberian peninsula, but the drawback is that they are much cooler than those on the Mediterranean coast. The climate here is temperate and humid. Winter weather is cold and wet and much more like the winters in the UK than on the Costa del Sol. Not surprisingly, despite the region's beauty and its low cost of living, very few foreigners have chosen to reside, or to buy a second home, here. In part because of this, the region is far less developed than the eastern coastline. Another factor is that the links to the UK and other European destinations are relatively poor. This coast is a popular tourist destination for many Spaniards during the summer.

Galicia is remarkably different from the rest of Spain. Cut off by mountains from the rest of Spain and from Portugal to the south, the region and its population are of Celtic origin and have much in common with Ireland and Brittany. The coastline is rugged and interspersed with small coves, sandy beaches and many natural harbours, often swept by storms and high winds. The land is green and fertile, and the economy heavily centred on agriculture and fishing. Rain is in good supply. The region has also suffered from economic emigration, with many Galicians seeking work in the UK. In many inland areas the primary language is Galego. Apart from this language, which has Latin roots close to those of Portuguese, the region has a rich heritage that is definitely Celtic.

The region is home to one of Spain's most historic and most beautiful cities, Santiago de Compostela, which is known in particular for its Romanesque cathedral, reputedly the burial place of the Apostle St. James, and attracts pilgrims from all parts of the Christian world.

Asturias is more Spanish, certainly in its language, although it too shares in a Celtic past. The region is green, its coast forming part of the Costa Verde, and pitted with bays and hidden coves. The economy is in large part agricultural, though the cities of Gijón and Oviedo were home to coal mining and shipbuilding. Asturias is reputed for its gastronomy, strong cheeses and cider. Inland the terrain is mountainous. The people here are fiercely independent, and for 200 years this was the only Christian region in an Iberian peninsula under Islamic rule.

Cantabria is also Spanish speaking, green and mountainous. It boasts delightful beaches, and popular tourist resorts in and around Santander, one of Spain's busiest ports and a major link to the rest of the world. The region is famous for its prehistoric sites. Its economy relies heavily on farming.

The Basque country has an identity that sets it apart from the rest of Spain. Its people are strongly independent in nature, and the separatist movement receives considerable support from the local population, though many remain opposed to the violent tactics of the ETA terrorists. The area centred around Bilbao, the sixth largest city in Spain, is one of the country's most industrialized. Elsewhere the landscape is green and the economy for the most part agricultural, or heavily forested. Spoken only by a minority, the Basque language (Euskera) is forcefully promoted by the regional authorities. Their efforts are not assisted by the complexities of the language. The people have a reputation for friendliness, and for excellent cuisine, centred around seafood.

Property prices are much, much lower throughout the region bordering the North Atlantic coast than on the Mediterranean coast, save in and around the university city of Santander in Cantabria, and the beautiful Basque city and cultural centre of San Sebastian towards the French border, a Spanish equivalent to Biarritz. A sizeable house near the coast, though not on the beach, should cost under 250,000 euros, and inland houses needing restoration with some land are available for under 60,000 euros.

Facilities on the northern coast are obviously much less developed than on Spain's Mediterranean coastline. Unless you chose to live in one of the larger cities, a car is essential. There is little in the way of leisure services outside the main towns and cities, save during the summer tourist season. As one might expect, various water sports are popular here including sailing, windsurfing, scuba diving, fishing along the coast, canoeing and fishing inland. Also popular inland are horse-riding and mountaineering. On the eastern side of the coast some of the ski resorts in the Pyrenees are within relatively easy reach. Cantabria, in particular, has a number of golf courses.

British and English-speaking contacts

There are very few facilities specifically catering for English speakers. There is one English school in Asturias and a US school in Bilbao. British and foreign foods are available in some larger stores, and the few specialist shops. As always the El Cortes Inglés department store is worth taking a look at. You will not find the British pubs and restaurants reminiscent of the Costa del Sol on this coast. The English-speaking population is small, and accordingly there is no local English radio station or newspaper.

The UK has consulates in Bilbao and Pontevedra, the Irish consulate is in Bilbao and the US consulate is in Coruna.

UK travel links

The most established links with the UK are the ferry services to Plymouth from Santander and Bilbao (summer only). The former takes about 24 hours, the latter nearly 36. The main airport in the north east is the international airport at Bilbao. There are also airports in Santander and Asturias but these cater for domestic flights only. The Labacolla airport near Santiago de Compostela has flights to several European capitals, including London. The main routes for scheduled flights are:

Biarritz: London Stansted

Bilbao: London Gatwick, London Heathrow, London Stansted

Santiago de Compostela: London Heathrow

Other travel information

There are train links between most of the larger cities and Madrid. The line along the northern coast is slow. The road links to Madrid are reasonably good, and work on a major road along the coast is due to be completed within the next 12 months.

The Balearic Islands

The Balearic Islands are to be found 200 kilometres to the south east of Barcelona. There are three main islands, Majorca, Minorca and Ibiza, and several smaller islands including Formentera. Catalan is spoken on all three islands, as well as Spanish, with a strong leaning towards Catalan in the inland and remoter areas.

The islands have long been a preferred holiday destination of northern Europeans. Of the foreign property buyers here the Germans are by far the greatest in number, with the British tending to prefer the mainland coast, especially the Costa del Sol. Nevertheless the British constitute the second largest contingent of foreigners on the islands, followed by the Scandinavians and the Dutch.

While the islands have much in common, there are significant differences, including even in their climate (Minorca, in particular, is subject to high winds), and in the extent to which they have been changed by the influx of tourists and foreign residents.

In December 2003 a massive coastal clean-up operation was announced. The programme, due to continue for two years, is to involve 15 boats and 22 smaller vessels and satellite equipment to locate the build up of rubbish, including plastic bags and bottles, to prevent contamination of bathing areas on the islands.

Majorca

Majorca ('ma-yorca') is the largest of the islands. It is about 95 kilometres at its widest point and has a population approaching 700,000, an increase of over 100,000 over the last 20 years. There is a substantial foreign presence here, with an estimated 25,000 British and probably a slightly higher number of German residents. The island, also known as the 'Isle of Dreams', is one of the most popular tourist destinations, welcoming over 3 million British and around 4 million German tourists each year. Not surprisingly, San Juan airport is the busiest in Spain and is set to handle in excess of 20 million passengers a year.

The island has a very varied terrain with much of the north west being dominated by the Sierra de Tramontana, a mountain range that boasts several peaks the height of Ben Nevis or above, the highest being Puig Mayor (1,445 metres). Inland the island is unspoilt, tranquil and rugged. On the coast you will find hidden coves with sandy beaches, and cliff faces where the mountains meet the sea. Much of the more accessible coastline is intensely developed.

Recent years have seen a move away from the unattractive high-rise hotels that were so characteristic of the early years of mass tourism on the island, with the local government imposing stricter regulations aimed at preserving the natural beauty of the island. A controversial 'eco-tax' was payable on stays in tourist accommodation, the income from which was used to finance a number of conservation-type schemes. This tax was unpopular and has been abolished. In the near future, at least, the island is unlikely to see anywhere near the scale of construction experienced over the last 40 years or so. Indeed, in some areas there is a current ban on further construction. There is a buoyant property market, and in the last four months of 2003 prices of property on the island increased by an average of 13.5 per cent.

The capital of Majorca, and the main administrative centre for the Balearic Islands, is Palma de Majorca in the Bay of Palma. It is home to nearly half of the island's inhabitants, and a substantial English-speaking community. The city is the main cultural centre on the island. Here you will find an extensive range of facilities and leisure activities including concerts, recitals, plays and exhibitions.

For the last three years Palma City Council, in conjunction with the Balearic Disabled Federation, has been assisting businesses finance the cost of adapting their premises to better meet the needs of the disabled. In Palma 80 premises and 6 streets have undergone alterations. It is hoped to extend the programme throughout the Balearic Islands.

The cost of living on the island is the highest in Spain. Property prices are similarly higher than elsewhere, though they vary considerably. The most expensive area is undoubtedly around Calvia, to the west of Palma, and also the area towards Andratx. Much lower-priced property can be found inland, and on the western side of Palma Bay. If you are interested in restoring a house in an inland village, you may be able to pick something up at around 125,000 euros. A two-bedroom apartment in the Bay of Palma is likely to cost around 160,000 euros. Villas on the island start from in excess of 450,000 euros. If you would feel happy living in a primarily British environment within Spain, consider the various developments in the resorts of Magalluf and Palma Nova, which tend to be British-dominated. As to rental accommodation, there is no difficulty in finding property for short-term lettings, though the opposite is true of longer term rentals. Public transport links between the main towns are good, but inland and to the north you will definitely need a car. The standard of the roads between main centres is also good, but this is not true inland.

Majorca enjoys hot summers. Winters are mild, especially on the coast. During the autumn and winter, especially, rain can be torrential.

The island has a huge variety of sporting and leisure activities. Water sports of all kinds are popular, but especially sailing. Golf is very popular – the island boasts five 18-hole golf courses – and also hiking. The island has all the facilities and amenities that you might expect for such a popular holiday destination, including various theme and water parks, and a vibrant nightlife. In summer the island is overflowing with tourists, a factor to bear in mind if you are considering purchasing in one of the more popular tourist areas. A further downside of the island's popularity is that it does attract crime. This is on the increase, primarily petty theft, and drunken hooliganism in and around the island's night spots during the summer months.

In Palma you will find an extensive range of shops and chain stores, as well as the department store El Corte Inglés. Elsewhere there is a plentiful supply of supermarkets and smaller shops.

Majorca also boasts many annual *fiestas*, in particular that of Saint John in June, and Saint Sebastian in Palma each January.

There is a university at Palma that has a variety of different courses of interest to foreigners (see below), as well as to the local population.

You will find useful information about the islands on the Web site of the Balearic Tourist Office site: www.visitbalearics.net and also on www.mallorcaweb.com

British and English-speaking contacts

There are four British schools on the island, including the Baleares International School and Queen's College, and one US school. There are also a number of private Catholic Spanish schools, but you should note that your child is likely to receive a bilingual education in Spanish and Catalan, as he or she would in a local state school. There is a plentiful supply of doctors who claim to speak English, and indeed many of them do. There is an Anglican Church in Palma (see its Web site www.anglican-mallorca.org) with services also at Cala d'Or, Cala Bona, Puerto Pollensa and Puerto Soller. There are also a good number of English-speaking clubs and associations, including bridge, cricket and theatre groups.

There is a cinema in Palma that has one film in English each week. British and some other foreign foods are stocked by the supermarkets, and also by a number of specialist shops. There are a significant number of British-style pubs and restaurants on the island.

The University of the Balearic Islands is based in Palma, and has an English version of its Web site. The address is www.uib.es/en. There is a daily English-language newspaper, *The Mallorca Daily Bulletin,* and one weekly publication, *The Reader.* The free regular publication *Santa Ponça Scene* is worth casting an eye over.

There is a British consulate on the island, as well as several other consulates including those of Ireland, the United States and Germany.

UK travel links

The main routes for scheduled flights are as follows.

Palma: Bristol, East Midlands, Leeds/Bradford, Liverpool, London Gatwick, London Heathrow, London Luton, London Stansted, Manchester

Falcon Holidays is set to start package holidays to the island in 2004 from City of Derry Airport, in Northern Ireland.

Other travel information

Links with mainland Spain are good, with flights to Madrid, Barcelona and Valencia. There are ferry links to Barcelona, Alicante, Valencia and also to Marseilles and Genoa as well as the other Balearic Islands. The ferries to mainland Spain take 8 to 10 hours, but there is a catamaran to Barcelona that takes 4 hours.

Minorca

The second largest of the Balearic Islands, Minorca, is 48 kilometres long and 15 kilometres wide. As is apparent from some of its architecture, the capital Mahón ('Georgetown') was under British rule intermittently from 1708 to 1782. It is very different from both Majorca and Ibiza, being much less developed and far more tranquil, even during the summer months. The population of the island, at just over 70,000, is a mere tenth of that on Majorca with around 3,000 to 4,000 foreign residents, mostly British and German.

Minorca has well over a hundred different beaches and a very mild climate, though it experiences strong winds from autumn well into spring. The island's resorts are concentrated on the south coast, with little development on the rocky northern coast. Water sports are popular, especially sailing, windsurfing and scuba diving. There is only one golf course on Minorca. The capital, Mahón, on the east coast, is a cultural centre with events throughout much of the year, though most of the rest of the island has little happening outside the summer months. If you want to party into the small hours this is not the island for you, and you should try Majorca or Ibiza.

Property prices are cheaper here than on the other Balearic Islands, save in the capital Mahón. Modest villas towards the coast start from about 225,000 euros, and apartments from about 100,000 euros with prices being lower on the west of the island. If you intend to purchase land on which to build, ensure that planning permission has already been obtained. Here, as on the other islands, the authorities have tightened building regulations and reduced the number of licences being granted. Considerable importance is now given to conserving the island's natural resources.

You will find useful information about the island on the Web site of the Balearic Tourist Office site: www.visitbalearics.net and also at www.menorcaweb.com

British and English-speaking contacts

British and other foreign food items are available from the larger supermarkets and some specialist shops. There is an English lending library in Mahon. There are no British or international schools on the island. There is no British consulate on the island. There is an Anglican church at Es Castell. There is one monthly English-language magazine, *Roquetta*, and a variety of clubs and associations, including a cricket club.

UK travel links

There is a small international airport just south of Mahon, operating scheduled flights to London Gatwick and London Luton.

Other travel information

There are charter flights from several European airports during the summer months. There are flights daily to the mainland and ferry links to Barcelona and Valencia, as well as to Majorca.

Ibiza

Ibiza (Eivissa) is much closer to the mainland than Majorca and Minorca (Valencia is only three hours away by ferry) and is about one-sixth the size of Majorca. It is characterized by stunning beaches, sheer cliff faces and tiny hidden coves. The island is home to nearly 95,000 inhabitants, with the foreign contingent mainly of Germans, and to a lesser extent Britons, estimated at over 15 per cent of the total population. A large number of Spaniards have also moved here. The population of the island has almost doubled in the last 25 years, and less than half the island's inhabitants were born on Ibiza.

Ibiza is perhaps *the* most popular holiday destination for young Britons and Germans intent on partying through the night. The raucous behaviour of many of these visitors has been accompanied by drunken violence and by crime. In recent years the demands on the time of the British vice-consulate have increased, visiting and advising those arrested by the local police.

The noisy nightlife is concentrated around the island's capital Ibiza Town and San Antonio, and to some extent Santa Eulàlia. You will find that most of the island is peaceful, and to a large extent undeveloped, its beauty unspoilt by the tourist-led construction boom of the 1960s.

Average temperatures here are slightly higher than on the other islands – 12°C in winter and 25°C in summer. There is a serious shortage of water on the island.

As on the other Balearic Islands, conditions and facilities for water sports are excellent. There is only one golf course. The cultural life of the island is concentrated in Ibiza Town and Santa Eulàlia. The island has two water parks. There is a medical centre in San Antonio.

For the most part property is more expensive here than on the other islands, with few villas available under 550,000 euros (800,000 euros on the coast). Apartments start at about 180,000 euros.

You will find useful information about the islands on the Web site of the Balearic Tourist Office site: www.visitbalearics.net and also at www.eivis-saweb.com

British and English-speaking contacts

British and other foreign food items are available from supermarkets and some specialist shops. There is one British school, the Morna International College in Sant Carles. *The Ibiza Sun* is a free weekly publication in English. Its Web site (www.theibizasun.net) includes a list of useful telephone numbers. There is a variety of clubs and associations, including sports and theatre groups. There is an Anglican church at San Antonio, and services also at Santa Eulàlia.

UK travel links

There is a small international airport with scheduled flights from the East Midlands and London Stansted, as well as many charter flights to a number of UK destinations.

Other travel information

There are many flights during summer months to Germany. At other times you are likely to have to fly via one of the mainland airports. There are ferry services to Barcelona, Valencia and Denia as well as to Majorca and the small neighbouring island of Formentera.

Formentera

Formentera is the smallest of the inhabited islands of the Balearics, and can only be reached by ferry from Ibiza. The island is almost completely undeveloped. You will find information about the islands on the Web site of the Balearic Tourist Office site: www.visitbalearics.net and also at www.formenteraweb.com

The Canary Islands

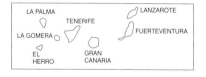

Situated about 100 kilometres off the coast of West Africa (parallel to the southernmost point of Morocco), and colonized by Spain in the 15th century, the Canary Islands are well over 1,000 kilometres from Spain. There are seven islands altogether: the main islands of Lanzarote, Fuerteventura, Gran Canaria, Tenerife, and the three smaller islands of La Palma, La Gomera and El Hierro. Together they enjoy a sub-tropical climate of all-year sunshine that has made them highly popular tourist destinations for northern

Europeans, including in the Victorian era. These volcanic islands have an amazing juxtaposition of landscapes, ranging from Spain's highest mountain, Pico del Teide (3,700 metres) on Tenerife, to deserts, jungle terrain and stunning beaches.

Property prices here are substantially cheaper than in the Balearic Islands, but more expensive than on mainland Spain. The climate is hotter throughout the year, but there is relief from the high summer temperatures (27°C is not uncommon) thanks to refreshing ocean breezes. A less welcome climatic feature is the occasional sandstorm from the Sahara that can last for several days, causing respiratory problems.

Though part of Spain, and hence of the European Union, the Canaries are not covered by the same taxation and customs regulations. Accordingly many products, including cars and electrical goods, are much cheaper here than elsewhere in Spain. Overall the cost of living is similar to other popular Spanish resorts. Tourism is the main industry on the islands, though there is a significant fishing industry. Vineyards and banana plantations also play an important part in the local economy. There are few job opportunities outside of tourism, and for those wishing to work in that sector an ability to get by in German and Spanish is a definite advantage, perhaps even essential. There is a shortage of water on the islands which explains the presence of various desalination plants. The islands' population of 1.7 million is concentrated mostly on Gran Canaria and Tenerife. Useful information about the islands can be found on the Web site for News Canarias at www.ic-web.com

Tenerife

The largest island is Tenerife with a population of around 700,000. It is the most popular of the Canary Islands for Britons buying property. Estimates of the number of foreign residents vary from 10 to 15 per cent of the total population, with the British and Germans being the most numerous. The capital and main cultural centre is Santa Cruz de Tenerife in the north of the island, visited by tens of thousands of cruise-ship passengers each year. The city is known for its extravagant carnival (the largest in Spain) that takes place each February.

The holiday resorts are concentrated along the west coast, which is considered to have the best climate. The most popular resorts are the noisy and bustling Playa de Las Américas, Los Cristianos, Puerto de la

Cruz and also the calmer resort of Los Gigantes. The beaches are all composed of grey volcanic sand, save for a recent development at Santa Cruz where golden sand was imported from the Sahara. The island boasts all the sports and leisure facilities that one would expect from a top tourist destination, with an emphasis on water sports. It has some of the best marinas in the world. Golf is also very popular with six golf courses, two of them (Amarilla Golf and Golf de Sur) being championship courses. There is an extensive range of cultural events and activities throughout most of the year, including theatre and musical concerts, primarily in the capital Santa Cruz. The shopping facilities are excellent and include several large supermarkets, a large El Corte Inglés store in Santa Cruz and even a branch of Ikea.

Geographically the island is split in two by its mountain range. The south is dry and arid. In complete contrast, the north is green with vegetation, including banana plantations, forests and beautiful flora. In the middle of the island the volcano Pico del Teide is said to be dormant, the last eruption being nearly a century ago.

Property prices have risen considerably over the past decade. For two-bedroom apartments, and inland rural properties, prices start at a little over 100,000 euros, and for a three-bedroom villa prices start at about 225,000 euros. There are significant price variations, however.

The local authorities are now restricting further development on the island. If you do decide to buy land on which to build, you should ensure that it has planning permission and that you are happy with any conditions placed on any proposed building.

British and English-speaking contacts

English-language films can be seen at the cinema complex in Los Cristianos, but only during the summer. British and other foreign foods are available in most supermarkets and indeed other shops, but they can be expensive. Pubs and restaurants offering British-style food are in plentiful supply. There are English-language church services for various denominations including Anglican churches in La Palma, Los Cristianos, Los Gigantes, Puerto Santiago, Playa de Las Américas and Puerto de la Cruz. There are three British schools on the island, and one private Spanish school. There are four English radio stations to tune into: Power FM, Radio Oasis, Gold FM and Waves FM, and several English-language publications. These include *Island Connections, Island Sun, The Paper* and *Tenerife News* (which has a useful Web site at www.tennews.com with a number of links). There is also a substantial number of British-run businesses operating on the island, including Mary's bookshop in Puerto de la Cruz, and the Book Swap in Las Américas.

UK travel links

There is scheduled flights from London Gatwick, London Luton and Manchester to the main airport of Reina Sofia in the south of the island (near the Costa del Silencio!). There are also a large number of charter flights to the UK.

Other travel information

There is a second airport at Los Rodeos. This is primarily for inter-island flights and flights to the mainland. There are extensive ferry services connecting Tenerife to the other Canary Islands. Los Cristianos is Spain's busiest port, in the last year registering over 1.3 million users. On the whole, the network of main roads connecting the larger towns and resorts on the island is good, as are the bus services between the larger population centres.

Gran Canaria

Gran Canaria is the third largest of the islands, but the second most populated with about 750,000 inhabitants, about half living in Las Palmas de Gran Canaria, the administrative capital of the Canary Islands. The island welcomes even more tourists than Tenerife, with the busiest resorts being on the southern coast that boasts several long beaches and amazing sand dunes, in particular at Maspalomas. There are a number of more peaceful resorts to the west of the island, where the coastline, like that in the north, is rugged. The centre of Gran Canaria is dominated by mountains and deep valleys with plantations of bananas, sugar cane and mango.

Substantial numbers of north Europeans have settled on the island, and there is a significant British community living here.

The island boasts a huge range of sports and leisure activities, including several theme and water parks. As with other island destinations, the emphasis is on water sports, especially sailing, and several regattas take place each year. There are various marinas, and deep-sea fishing and scuba diving are popular. In addition, there are five golf courses. There is a busy cultural calendar of events in Las Palmas, embracing musical concerts, opera, theatre and music. The capital, like the island's southern resorts, has a busy nightlife throughout much of the year. There are excellent shopping facilities, including the El Corte Inglés department store.

In recent years the rate of increase of property prices on Gran Canaria has slowed. Prices are still high, however. Two-bedroom apartments start from about 120,000 euros and villas from about 300,000 euros. The more expensive areas are at Maspalomas, Playa del Inglés and San Augustin. If you intend to buy land as a building plot, check that planning permission has already been granted, and that you are happy with any conditions attached to the grant.

British and English-speaking contacts

There are two British schools and one US school on the island. In addition to several public hospitals there is a British hospital and several private clinics. English-language publications include *Island Connections, Island Sun, The Paper* and *Tenerife News*. At the time of writing, there were no showings of English films, although there were plans to introduce these. British and foreign foods are stocked in most of the larger supermarkets, although prices can be expensive. There is an Iceland store on the island. A substantial number of pubs, bars and restaurants on the island offer British fare. Many of them are owned by expatriates. There are several other types of British-run businesses. There is an Anglican church in Las Palmas, and services at Playa de Inglés.

The British consulate is in Las Palmas, along with consulates for Ireland, the United States, South Africa and Germany.

UK travel links

From London, there are flights from Gatwick. There are charter flights from the UK throughout much of the year. The airport is on the east coast at Gando, and several million visitors a year pass through it.

Other travel information

There are regular flights to mainland Spain, and ferry services to the other islands and to Spain.

Lanzarote

Lanzarote, the fourth largest island, is the hottest and most arid. It is the least developed of the larger Canary Islands. Arrecife, the capital, is not particularly attractive. The main tourist centres are at Puerto del Carmen, south of the capital, and Playa Blanca, which is further south still, at the southern-most tip. The island is famous for its mountainous volcanic landscape, and numerous extinct volcanoes in the Timanfaya National Park, as well as both its white and grey sandy beaches.

Building has been restricted in the past, and this is likely to remain the case as the authorities strive to avoid the overcrowding and the unattractive constructions that are to be seen in parts of Gran Canaria and Tenerife. One-bedroom apartments start at about 80,000 euros and villas from about 340,000 euros.

The population of the island is only about 65,000 with substantial British and German contingents.

The island has fewer sports and leisure opportunities than Gran Canaria and Tenerife, but offers an ample selection of water sports, including wind surfing, scuba diving and deep-sea fishing. A major sports complex is due to open within the next few years. The island has a selection of shopping centres.

British and English-speaking contacts

There are two British schools on the island and several private Catholic Spanish schools. There is a private hospital aimed primarily at the foreign residents, and two public hospitals. There are Anglican services in Arrecife, at Costa Teguise, Playa Blanca, Golf del Sur and Puerto del Carmen, and also Baptist and Evangelical services on the island. English-language publications include *Island Connections, Island Sun, The Paper.*

UK travel links

There are many charter flights to the UK. Falcon Holidays is set to start package holidays to the island in 2004 from Derry City Airport in Northern Ireland.

Other travel information

There are ferry services to the other islands.

Fuerteventura

Fuerteventura is the second largest island, but one of the least populated with about 55,000 inhabitants, including substantial British and German communities. The island boasts long white sandy beaches. It is very arid with little rainfall or vegetation, a substantial part of the island constituting desert. It is undeveloped, peaceful and unspoilt. The main resorts are on the eastern side of the island, to the south of the capital Puerto del Rosario and on the Jandia peninsula at the southern tip of the island.

The island has limited amenities compared to Gran Canaria and Tenerife, but an extensive selection of water sports including surfing, windsurfing, sailing, scuba diving and deep-sea fishing. There is one golf course.

Property prices on Fuerteventura are lower than elsewhere in the Canaries, but are increasing at a faster rate. Two-bedroom apartments start from about 135,000 euros and villas from about 240,000.

British and English-speaking contacts

British food items are available in the resort supermarkets, though they tend to be quite expensive. There is no British or private schooling on Fuerteventura, nor are there any public or private hospitals. English-language publications include *Island Connections, Island Sun* and *The Paper.*

UK travel links

There are regular charter flights to the UK throughout the summer.

Other travel information

There is a regular ferry service to Gran Canaria.

La Palma, La Gomera and El Hierro

These are the three smallest islands. La Palma has the largest population at about 80,000 with La Gomera and El Hierro having 18,000 and 6,000 inhabitants respectively. There are significant numbers of foreigners living on all three islands, in particular Germans, but relatively few Britons. All three islands have largely avoided mass tourism, with La Gomera and El Hierro being particularly unspoilt.

La Palma is characterized by lush vegetation, thick woodlands, a vast volcanic crater, a mountain range reaching to a height of nearly 2,500 metres (almost twice the height of Ben Nevis), and an active volcano that last erupted 30 years ago. Its capital Santa Cruz de la Palma was a port of major importance in the Spanish Empire. The town still has a colonial ambience. La Gomera also has its mountain range, with its highest peaks reaching almost 1,500 metres. It too boasts lush vegetation, including rain forests. El Hierro has the smallest population of the inhabited islands. It is seldom visited by tourists, and agriculture is its main economic activity.

There are relatively few amenities on any of these three islands, with none of them yet possessing a golf course. Trekking, pot-holing, and scuba diving are popular in La Palma. Sailing and scuba diving are popular on La Gomera and El Hierro.

All three islands have a selection of supermarkets, especially La Palma and La Gomera. A limited range of British food items are available on the islands. There are no international or private schools on any of the islands. All three have hospitals, although the cover available at El Hierro, in particular, is limited. In La Palma there is an English-language version of the monthly magazine *Informagazin*.

The cost of housing has risen in recent years on all three islands. The cheapest prices are on La Gomera and El Hierro where two-bedroom apartments are available from about 90,000 euros. On La Palma prices are still lower than on the four larger Canary Islands.

UK travel links

There are no direct flights from the UK, and for all three islands you will need to fly first to Tenerife or Gran Canaria, save that for La Palma there are flights via Madrid.

Other travel information

La Palma has a tiny airport suitable for small aircraft only. There are daily flights to Tenerife and Gran Canaria, and flights to Madrid, Amsterdam and some German locations. From La Gomera and El Hierro there are flights only to Tenerife and Gran Canaria. There are a number of ferry services linking these islands to Tenerife and Gran Canaria.

Madrid

The Spanish capital is situated almost in the centre of the country, on a high plateau 600 metres above sea level. With a population of 3 million, Madrid is by far the largest city in Spain, the centre of a huge manufacturing area and the wealthiest region in Spain. It is a major cultural centre with an abundance of museums, theatres, majestic buildings, busy nightlife and leisure facilities, and a smooth-running and inexpensive transport system.

The city is constantly busy from early morning until the small hours. Despite its excellent public transport network, it suffers from traffic congestion, impossible parking conditions, pollution and noise. As in any large city, petty crime, especially theft, is commonplace, with tourists often the targets.

The climate in Madrid can be summed up in one word: fierce. The city has a continental climate with summers being stiflingly hot, and the winters bitterly cold.

The cost of living in Madrid is much lower than in other European capitals. Property prices, though higher here than in many other areas of Spain, are also significantly lower than in, say, London or Paris, with two-bedroom apartments starting at about 220,000 euros. The city has a large population of foreign residents, mainly from Africa and South America, but also several thousand English speakers, mostly British or American, and a significant French population. The latter nationalities tend to favour living in the centre of the city, to the north, or the new towns that have been constructed on the outskirts. For the most part they avoid the suburbs to the south.

On the outskirts of Madrid, the leisure opportunities include golf on one of the many excellent courses, and skiing in the mountains close by. Sites worth visiting include the science museum and planetarium and the city's zoo, not to mention the Madrid amusement park, several water parks and Warner Brothers' Movieworld, a recently opened theme park to the south of the capital.

As one would expect, shopping facilities in Madrid are first-class, though the selection of British food products is very limited. As always El Corte Inglés is worth a visit.

British and English-speaking contacts

There are two publications serving the English-speaking population: *The Broadsheet* and *Guidepost,* both free monthly magazines distributed at key points around the city. There are many British and other native English speakers running a host of different types of businesses in the city. These include a small number of doctors and dentists who have set up in practice here. There is an apparently free pregnancy and birth advisory service that I have seen advertised. The advertisement states that it is run by an English-speaking childbirth educator. The two public hospitals with the best reputations are Hospital de la Paz and the Hospital Doce de Octubre.

There are several international schools in Madrid, including British schools and one US school, and of course many private Spanish schools mostly offering a Catholic education. The city's universities include the Schiller International University that offers a number of business related degree programmes (Web site: www.schillermadrid.edu/). There are a number of cinemas that show films in English, as well as several book-shops selling English-language books. The city has an Anglican church (St George's), as well as Baptist, Methodist and Presbyterian churches and the international inter-denominational Community Church of Madrid. There are also Catholic services in English.

The capital has an extensive array of clubs and associations established by English-speaking expatriates, embracing sports, social groups, theatre, politics, a Canadian association, a South African association, Scottish country dancing, a cricket club, a British football team that plays in a local Spanish league, a Lions Rugby Club. There is even a charity shop run by the British Ladies Association. Friendly watering holes include Finnegan's pub, Café Madrid (metro Opera), and Planet Hollywood in Plaza de las Cortes.

UK and Ireland travel links

There are direct flights to: Birmingham, Dublin, Liverpool, London Gatwick, London Heathrow, London Luton.

Other travel information

As one would expect, there are direct flights to many international destinations as well as the main provincial airports. The efficient public transport system includes an underground rail network.

3 Renting a home in Spain

Reasons to rent

Purchasing a property in Spain is a serious business. While property prices are generally lower than in the UK (notable exceptions being in parts of the Costa del Sol), acquisition costs are higher. Similarly, costs when you come to sell are appreciably more. Choosing the wrong property or the wrong location will be an expensive mistake. Once you have purchased, you may not be able to sell and purchase elsewhere for some considerable time. Accordingly, you should give serious consideration to renting a property before you buy. Even if you know the area in which you intend to purchase well, living somewhere is naturally very different from the occasional holiday, particularly if your holidays have all been during the summer months. Renting, whether a furnished or unfurnished property, will give you the time to look around, consider your options and decide if the area does indeed fit your requirements after all.

In deciding whether to rent or buy you will need to consider:

- whether or not you have sufficient finances to cover the initial outlay of purchasing and can afford the monthly instalments;
- the size of the property you require – it is likely that you will be able to afford to rent a larger property than you will be able to buy and, in the short to medium term, this may suit your plans better than buying;
- the rental market – in some areas, the rental property market can be very limited, with far greater choice being available to those able to purchase their own home;
- whether or not the size of your family is likely to change over the following years;
- your job security and the availability of insurance for loss of employment;

- your age – it is obviously preferable to purchase prior to age 45 in order to be able to pay off your mortgage before retirement;
- whether or not your job is likely to require you to move and to what extent your employers will cover relocation costs;
- the likely rate of growth in the value of property in your chosen location – the value of a flat on the Costa del Sol is likely to rise faster than the value of a house in the remoter parts of Spain, for example;
- how much time you have available to carry out your research – the purchase of a property inevitably calls for more expenditure of time than does choosing a property to rent;
- whether you wish to tie up the capital required for the purchase of your property;
- any implications for your tax position;
- your wishes in relation to the passing on of the property purchased in the event of your death.

I would strongly recommended that anyone moving to Spain should rent initially, if only for a period of a year or so. It enables you to familiarize yourself with the locality and the various amenities (or lack of them). It allows you the opportunity to get to know an area and some of the local population. Far better to read in the local paper about protests about a planned new road or other major development while you are renting, than after you have sunk your hard-earned savings into what turns out to be a living nightmare. It also permits you to search around for an attractively priced property and to take advantage of any bargain that may come onto the market. One disadvantage, especially in an area like the Costa del Sol, is that prices are constantly rising. If you rent for too long, you may jeopardize your purchasing power.

I would also strongly recommend that you do not enter into a rental agreement before arriving at your destination in Spain. Instead, book two weeks or so in short-term or holiday accommodation. If you are intending to rent for only a year or less, do give consideration to a furnished letting.

Finding a home to rent

There are many different publications and Web sites (such as www.hispavista.com and www.segundamano.es) specializing in Spain and the Spanish property market, where you will find details of properties for rent, many of them being let by fellow Britons who have already purchased a holiday home in Spain. Once in Spain, you will find advertisements in most of the local newspapers, but also in the local English-language press (for details see under each region in Chapter 2). When answering these advertisements, take precautions. Ask as many questions as you can over the telephone before embarking on what may prove to be a totally wasted visit. You may be responding to an advertisement by an agent who is advertising an attractive, but non-existent property merely to persuade readers to ring in. Often they will not supply any information by post, are reluctant to discuss details over the telephone and insist on you attending their offices. Reputable estate agents, however, can often prove very helpful.

Visiting the property

Insist on visiting the property at least twice, preferably on different days of the week, at different times and, if possible, in different weather conditions. Watch out for any signs on nearby properties suggesting that building or renovation works are planned.

Rental contracts

There are two main types of rental contract (*contrato de alquiler* or *contracte de lloguer* in Catalan). These are the *par temporada* (a short-term or seasonal contract) and *vivienda* (a long-term contract). A *par temporada* contract covers all holiday lettings and lettings up to a maximum of one year. After the expiry of the letting period, subject of course to any renewal, the tenant must leave. As in the UK and other European countries, tenants of such short-term lettings have little protection. These lettings are frequently of furnished properties, and the agreement should include an itemized inventory listing the contents of the property.

Protection afforded by Spanish law

The rental market for long-term lettings is subject to regulation by Spanish law, which protects, in particular, the tenant's right to stay in the property and, to a certain extent, the level of rent. Where there is a conflict between the written agreement between the parties and Spanish law, the law prevails.

Under the present Law of Urban Lettings (*Ley de Arrendamientos Urbanos*), in force since 1 January 1995, the law provides that in contracts *de vivienda*, ie rental contracts for one year or more, the tenant has an automatic right to renew the tenancy for up to five years. Accordingly, if you enter into a two-year agreement with a property owner, you have a right to remain in the property for up to a further three years. During this five-year period the landlord is entitled to increase the rent each year, but only in line with inflation. Once the five-year period has expired, the landlord then has the freedom to increase the rent as he or she wishes.

Short-term holiday rentals, *arrendamiento de temporada*, are not protected by this legislation. Unless stated to the contrary, this chapter deals with long-term lettings, although much of the practical advice is pertinent also to short-term or seasonal lettings.

There is also nothing to stop you entering into an agreement in English, and this is frequently done for self-catering holiday flats. A landlord wishing to let on a longer-term basis, however, cannot escape the protection granted by Spanish law by granting a tenancy in English, even if the agreement is signed by a UK tenant in the UK prior to leaving for Spain.

The rental agreement

Read this carefully! Consider having it checked over by an *abogado*. Agreements can be oral, but you should insist on a written contract confirming the tenancy and setting out the terms. The agreement should include the names of the proprietor and the tenant, the date the tenancy commences and its length. It must also give a description of the property, the level of rent, the amount of the deposit and purpose for which the property is being let. It is a good idea to register your rental contract with the local housing department.

The deposit (*fianza*)

A deposit of one month's rent is payable on the signing of the rental agreement. The proprietor may be prepared to give you more time to pay this – for example, taking half when you move into the property and half a month later. In any event, ask for a receipt. The deposit is paid as a guarantee of the condition of the property and the other risks taken by the proprietor in letting the property. At the end of the rental, the deposit is returned to the tenant, less the proprietor's costs of rectifying any damage to the property and any unpaid rent.

The deposit can be paid to an agency rather than the landlord. The agency should not release the deposit to either party without the consent of them both. I strongly recommend that you pay your deposit to a reputable estate agent or other agent, rather than to the landlord. An alternative is for the deposit to be held by the housing department of the regional government.

The length of the tenancy

The tenant is not obliged to stay up until the five-year permitted maximum, but he or she has a right to stay for the entire period. The proprietor cannot compel a tenant to leave before the end of the agreement except on limited grounds (primarily non-payment of rent and causing damage to the property, but also subletting without permission, disturbing neighbours, etc). In all cases a landlord must obtain a court order before evicting a tenant. This process can take a considerable time. In relation to rent arrears a tenant will be given time to pay, and a tenant will usually have to be several months in arrears before an order for possession will be made. As in the UK, the emphasis is on protecting the occupation of the tenant, providing he or she comes up with reasonable proposals to clear the arrears.

Community fees and taxes

Proprietors of apartments often insert terms into rental contracts requiring the tenant to pay the annual charges levied by the property owners' collective for the block, and sometimes the property tax or *impuesto sobre bienes inmuebles* (IBI). These fees and taxes can be substantial. While there is nothing to stop landlords trying to recover these expenses from a tenant in this way, the courts take a dim view of such attempts. Judges have struck out many such clauses as abusive, and tenants who feel that they have been unfairly pushed into agreeing to such clauses can often escape liability to pay the fees and IBI. Needless to say, if the fees and IBI are not mentioned in the rental agreement, the tenant is not obliged to pay them.

Maintenance of the property

This is the tenant's responsibility. His or her liability extends to minor repairs as well as maintenance in order to prevent the property falling into disrepair. The tenant's responsibility covers replacing broken windows, broken keys, paintwork, bleeding of radiators, replacement of bulbs, fuses and light fittings. The proprietor, on the other hand, remains responsible for substantial works of maintenance and repair.

Improvements to the property

The tenant does not need permission to carry out minor works, such as the fitting of a carpet in an unfurnished property. However, he or she is not entitled to carry out any substantial work or make holes in walls, for example, without the written consent of the proprietor.

The proprietor's right to carry out works

You are unlikely to be able to object to any necessary work that the proprietor wishes to carry out to maintain or improve the property. If peace and quiet are important to you (especially if you are at home during working hours) it would be wise to obtain the proprietor's written confirmation that no works of improvement will be carried out during the tenancy, save with your agreement. This should be recorded on the rental contract.

Insurance

A tenant should ensure that a policy of insurance is in force from the moment that he or she is in possession of the keys. Agreements frequently contain a provision allowing the proprietor to withdraw from the agreement if no insurance is in force.

Subletting

A tenant cannot sublet an apartment without the prior written consent of the proprietor. Even if as tenant you are given permission to sublet, you remain liable to pay any rent not paid by your sub-tenant.

If you are offered a sub-tenancy, you should ensure that the proprietor's written consent has been obtained or, preferably, enter into an agreement directly with him or her. If you do not, and the proprietor becomes entitled to end the tenancy he or she has granted to your landlord, you may well be left high and dry.

Notice to leave given by the landlord

If a landlord wishes to obtain possession of his or her property after the five years period has expired, he or she must notify the tenant (in writing, from a notary) well before the expiry of the five-year period. Failure to do so can mean that the tenancy is extended for a further two years on the same terms. Even if the landlord has given the requisite notice, he or she cannot simply proceed to evict the tenant – he or she must first obtain a court order for possession.

Before you move in

It is essential that a record of the state of the premises is completed before you move in. This is vital if you wish to reduce the risks of a nasty surprise when you come to leave, such as the proprietor blaming you for damage that was already present before you moved into the property. I recommend that you attend the property before you move in, preferably with the landlord or his or her representative, armed with the checklist supplied at the end of this chapter, and go through this document on site.

Check that the cooker and any machines included in the letting are in working order.

I suggest that you use a carbon to make two copies or each make your own copy of the completed document. Ensure that they are identical before both signing them. If only one copy is completed and signed, insist on providing the photocopy yourself. If you give the only copy to the landlord, you may cause yourself considerable problems if he or she loses it or otherwise fails to supply you with your copy.

I also strongly recommend that, on moving in, you take a video of the property, paying attention to any particular defects, and post this to yourself by recorded delivery so that you can prove the date that the video was taken. Do not open it unless some dispute arises at the end of the tenancy, in which case open it in front of some third party, such as an *abogado*, who can vouch for the fact that the envelope was previously unopened.

When you come to leave

A further record of the condition of the property should be completed and a comparison made with the previous one, to determine the extent of any damage caused during your occupation. I recommend that you make a video of the premises before leaving. In the middle of the recording, video a significant news item on the television or that day's newspaper so you can prove that it was not taken earlier.

Resolving disputes

In the event of a disagreement with the proprietor (for example, he or she is refusing to carry out a landlord's repair, or refusing to repay the deposit) you should seek advice. Obviously, instructing a lawyer can be expensive and may be out of proportion to the financial value of the dispute. There are, however, various agencies that provide free advice, including those that represent tenants' rights. A starting place is the *Oficina Municipal de Información al Consumidor.* This agency is charged with handling a wide range of consumer problems, as well as complaints relating to lettings. People with complaints about short-term or tourist occupation should contact the local tourist office.

Right of first refusal

As a tenant of a long-term letting you are entitled to first refusal should the proprietor put the property up for sale (this is referred to as the *tanteo y retracto,* the right of first refusal). The landlord should notify you, in writing, of the sale price, and the conditions of sale. If the landlord fails to do this, the tenant has the right to have the sale annulled, and to purchase the property at the price recorded on the contract for sale.

CHECKLIST ON MOVING IN/OUT: SPANISH

INQUILINO

PROPRIETARIO

PROPRIEDAD

FECHA

1 = muy bueno   2 = bueno   3 = pasable   4 = pobre

	pintura, suelo, techo, puertas vidrio ventana, persianas	electricidad armario modulo baño	instalación de agua metales	cerrraduras trabajo en
Sala				
Cocina				
Dormitorio 1				
Dormitorio 2				
Dormitorio 3				
Baño				
Cuarto de baño				
Entrada				
Sotano				
Garaje				

CHECKLIST ON MOVING IN/OUT: ENGLISH

TENANT:

PROPRIETOR:

PROPERTY:

DATE OF MOVING IN:

1 = very good   2 = good   3 = passable   4 = poor

room	paintwork ceiling window- panes	floor doors windows blinds	electricity	cupboards/ storage units	plumbing toilet installations	units
Living-room						
Kitchen						
Bed 1						
Bed 2						
Bed 3						
Toilet						
Bathroom						
Hall/entrance way						
Cellar						
Garage						

4 The purchase of your Spanish home

The first step: deciding on legal advice

Once you have decided to purchase a property in Spain, you should seriously consider consulting a lawyer before you even start your search. Legal advice should cover the various ways in which you can own your Spanish property, the options for mortgage finance and Spanish inheritance and tax rules.

The Spanish *notario* and the UK solicitor

The Spanish *notario* is very different from the English solicitor. The *notario* is, above all, a publicly appointed official. The main function of a *notario* is to draft legal documents, to see that the parties comply with relevant regulations, to inform the parties of their tax liabilities arising from the sale and purchase, and to verify that all monies have been paid. The *notario* does **not** carry out the important pre-contract enquiries that a UK solicitor would normally do.

In Spain you may well be assured by an estate agent that you have no need to appoint a lawyer, as the *notario* will carry out all the necessary work. This is not so. You should appoint your own lawyer. You would not dream of purchasing a property in the UK without instructing your own legally qualified representative, and you should adopt exactly the same approach to buying a property in Spain, where, if anything, the problems facing the unwary are greater.

It is also important that the lawyer you instruct should have knowledge of both Spanish *and* UK taxation and inheritance law, as well as Spanish property law. There are *notaires* in Spain, particularly in the areas most popular with UK house-buyers, who speak English very well and have acquired some knowledge of English law and procedures. Whether any of them have detailed knowledge of Scottish, Northern Irish or Irish law I question. In addition, there are some UK lawyers who have chosen to specialize in this area and some of them have obtained qualifications in Spanish law. They have the advantage of being able to communicate with you in English. There are also a few Spanish lawyers who have moved to the UK, are dually qualified and represent clients purchasing property in Spain. English-speaking Spanish lawyers can also be instructed via All about Spain Limited, which has a network of Spanish lawyers in both mainland Spain and the Balearic and Canary Islands. Their details, and contact details of lawyers in the UK and Spain, can be found in Appendix 1.

One further option is to instruct both a UK lawyer *and* a Spanish lawyer. Formed by barrister Kerrie Cox, following problems he encountered in the purchase of his own home in Spain, lawyers4spanish-homes.com/ offers such a service, at an overall cost of about 1 per cent of the purchase price plus VAT. Clients are put in contact with one of a team of Spanish lawyers, who with the assistance of translation software, keep the client up to date with the progress of their purchase via the Internet. In addition, clients have speedy access to an English barrister who can advise in relation to issues of English law, such as inheritance, and who will explain any questions or problems encountered during the transaction, and follow up any concerns with his or her Spanish counterpart.

I should emphasize that I have no personal interest in encouraging you to instruct your own lawyer to represent your interests. My firm advice, however, is that you should obtain legal advice from a lawyer familiar with the laws and regulations of both systems. Whichever route you take, obtain a prior written estimate of their fees, setting out how their charges will be calculated (usually a percentage of the property price subject to a minimum charge or an hourly rate). UK solicitors often charge 1 per cent of the purchase price (plus a further fee if they draft Spanish wills).

Methods of owning property

This is one area where advice is most definitely appropriate and should be obtained fairly early on in the formulation of your plans. There are several options available, each with different financial consequences, including what happens with regard to the passing on of the property in the event of your death and inheritance tax liabilities.

The options include joint ownership and purchasing through an offshore company. With the latter, when you wish to sell the property, you can simply sell the shares in the company. The purchaser makes a substantial saving on the acquisition costs (there is no taxable transfer of the property, only a transfer of the shares). This enables you to negotiate a better price with the purchaser. It can also mean that you could avoid Spanish inheritance tax. On the other hand, conscious of a loss of revenue, the Spanish government has put an *annual* tax of 3 per cent on property held by offshore companies.

An additional option, that you may be offered by a developer, is to buy under a leaseback scheme. Here, in contrast to a timeshare (see below) the purchaser acquires a legal interest in the property, is generally permitted to occupy it for several weeks a year, and eventually will obtain sole possession of the property. In brief, the purchaser buys the property at a discounted price, but agrees to lease the property back to the owner or a related company for several years, during which he or she is entitled to occupy the property for only a set period each year. After the end of the leaseback he or she is in the same position as someone who has purchased the property in the usual way. This may be a convenient way in which to purchase a retirement home 10 years or so before you come to retire.

Régimen matrimonial

On marriage Spaniards choose to adopt one of two regimes to govern their financial affairs. Many opt for common ownership of assets (*comunidad de bienes*) where everything acquired after marriage belongs to both spouses, even if held in the name of only one of them. Alternatively they can choose *separación de bienes* in which each spouse owns his or her own individual and separate assets. The latter regime is closest to the position in English law, where generally property is owned separately unless stated otherwise, as is usually the case in relation to a matrimonial home in the United Kingdom or a couple's joint bank account.

On the purchase of a property the notary will ask you your matrimonial regime, which he then records on the official documents. Most

Britons in Spain prefer to follow the UK system, and accordingly often request the notary to record that they have no matrimonial regime, but were married under English, Scottish or Irish law in which the system is similar to the regime of *separación de bienes*. Ask your lawyer to advise on which is the most appropriate for your particular circumstances.

Timeshares

Despite the fact that many of the worst 'horror' stories in the Spanish property market relate to timeshare schemes, they remain highly popular. Fortunately, regulations have now been introduced in Spain to comply with EU requirements.

In a timeshare scheme the purchaser buys the right to the use of the property for a limited period each year, often only a week or two. The buyer gains *no* legal interest in the property. The price is understandably much less than purchasing a holiday home, as are the maintenance costs. The developer, on the other hand, invariably makes a much higher profit than on a usual sale, as he or she will probably only have to sell a few weeks' use of the property to break even. Further, the service company responsible for the management of the development generally succeeds in levying much higher charges than on a normal development. With charges for each apartment shared between several 'owners', the time-share owners tend to pay over-inflated rates, rather than entering into conflict with the service company and risk losing their allocated time.

Most timeshare agreements are entered into during a 'presentation' when the prospective purchaser is subjected to extreme 'hard-sell'. Once the agreement was signed the purchaser had no opportunity to escape from the agreement, the contract was entirely weighted in favour of the developer and the service company, and further provided that disputes between the parties were subject to the law of some obscure tax haven.

The regulations now require a 10-day cooling off period after signature of the contract, during which you are entitled to withdraw from the agreement without penalty (though you must follow the correct procedure to do this). No deposit may be taken from you during this period.

The contract must be in the purchaser's own language, and he or she must be provided with correct information. If there is a discrepancy between the true position and the contract, or the publicity material

supplied, the purchaser is allowed an additional three months in which he or she can rescind the contract without cost to him- or herself. If the purchaser has taken out a loan to buy his or her timeshare, this is automatically cancelled also.

Disputes between the parties are to be decided according to Spanish law, the service companies must be registered in Spain and proprietors can be held responsible for the failings of the service company. A contract can still provide that failure to pay maintenance charges results in the loss of all your rights in the timeshare without compensation, and you should not agree to such a clause.

While buying a timeshare is much cheaper than purchasing your own apartment or house, you should nevertheless seriously consider consulting a lawyer before signing any agreement. The new regulations provide considerable protection, but the operators of timeshare companies are constantly making changes to their schemes in an effort to avoid the regulations, and the law is often too slow to keep up. These efforts often include conjuring up new names for their schemes, with such terms as 'vacation plans' and 'holiday ownership' now in current usage.

Before considering a timeshare purchase, at the very least consult the Timeshare Consumers' Association Web site at www.timeshare.org.uk. or telephone them on 01909 591 100.

Finding a property and negotiating with the vendor

There is a substantial amount of property available in Spain. This is partly owing to its low population density (Spain is four times the size of England, for example, but its population is very much less). It is also because the last 20 years have seen substantial movements away from rural areas to the main towns and cities.

Property is generally priced much lower than in the UK, save perhaps on parts of the Costa del Sol. You should be prepared to negotiate. Vendors in popular areas often put an asking price on their property well above what any local purchaser might contemplate, waiting in the hope of selling to a foreign buyer who doesn't know any better. Also note that the estate agent's commission is usually included in the sale price, and generally an agent will agree to lower his or her rather high commission rates in order to secure a sale.

FERNANDO SCORNIK GERSTEIN

Spanish Lawyers
(abogados, lawyers, rechtsanwalt, counsellors at law)

Specialists in:
litigation ▪ company and commercial law ▪
immigration ▪ conveyancing ▪ tax law ▪
investments ▪ probate ▪ personal injury ▪
matrimonial and family law ▪ criminal law ▪
intellectual property and maritime law.
Fiscal representation in Spain.

Branches in:
Madrid, Barcelona, Gran Canaria (2),
Lanzarote and Tenerife

Holborn Hall, 193-197 High Holborn
London WC1V 7BD, UK
Tel. 020 7404 8400
Fax: 020 7404 8500
E-mail: cedillo@fscornik.co.uk

Always bear in mind that some day, perhaps rather sooner than you might like, you will want to sell this property. You are more likely to be able to dispose of it easily if it is the type of property that would appeal to potential Spanish, as well as foreign, buyers. While property prices in Spain have tended to rise steadily, acquisition costs and sale costs (if you use an agent) are higher than in the UK, and in the *short* term residential property for owner occupation is unlikely to be a lucrative financial investment. Remember, too, that much of inland Spain can be cold during the winter months and so the larger the house, the higher your heating bills. While derelict properties are inexpensive, renovation costs are high and it is important to work out a realistic estimate of the likely total cost of your purchase.

Recent years have seen the appearance of a number of specialist magazines aimed at prospective UK house buyers. The articles in these publications are frequently helpful and informative. They also contain various advertisements by lawyers who are dually qualified and can provide legal advice in English, as well as estate agents who have set up agencies in Spain to assist English-speaking purchasers in their search for a dream home. They contain small advertisements from Britons, too, now wishing to sell their Spanish home without incurring an agent's fees or from the more adventurous Spanish vendors.

You will also find a selection of such advertisements in the quality UK newspapers, such publications as *The Lady* or even *Exchange & Mart*, and the Internet is also a convenient and frequently used means of locating properties in Spain.

Of course there are numerous exhibitions of Spanish property in London and elsewhere. Here you will be offered subsidized inspection trips. While this may be a convenient way to visit properties, you will only be taken to see a restricted range of properties on the particular agent's books, and often you will be obliged to put up with very 'hard sell'.

You could seek the services of an estate agent. This is the most popular method among the British. Estate agents vary in the quality of the service they provide, but many are extremely helpful and can provide practical information relating both to the properties they offer and the local area. You should supply the agent with as much detail as possible as to your requirements. An estate agent's commission is high (usually between 5 per cent and 10 per cent), and is included in the purchase price.

At present there are no legal regulations governing estate agents, and anyone may set him- or herself up as a property agent. The more reputable agents belong to either the *Agente de la Propriedad Inmobiliaria* (API) or to *Gestor Intermediario de Promociones y Edificaciones* (GIPE), both professional associations that require their members to meet certain standards. You should enquire of the agent whether he or she has professional indemnity insurance, and, if you are contemplating paying the deposit to him or her, whether he or she has a bonded client account. This is an account from which the money cannot be withdrawn, save for the purpose of the planned transaction. My advice, however, is that you should only pay the deposit to your lawyer.

There are also several UK-based estate agents. Generally, the UK agents carry out searches of properties being offered by a large number of Spanish agents over a wide area to identify properties that might be of particular interest to prospective UK purchasers. They prepare particulars and photographs. They may share the Spanish agent's commission, there then being no extra cost to the vendor (or purchaser). On the other hand, extra (hidden) commission is often charged. The agent does this by advertising the property at a price above the vendor's asking price and taking the difference as commission. Ask for a breakdown of the sale price and the different agents' commissions. This may enable you to negotiate a lower price. If you feel that the agent is not being frank, ask for the contact details of the Spanish agent and the vendor.

Do not assume that advice and information given to you by those with a financial interest in the sale of the property, whatever their nationality, is accurate or indeed truthful.

In rural areas, properties are often not advertised at all but are sold by word of mouth. If you have set your heart on a particular rural area, you could also make enquiries in the local shops or bars.

It is common practice for the vendor or his or her agent to present you with a *pre-contrato de compraventa*, or pre-contract document, for signature and to request a deposit of several thousand euros. The advantage to a purchaser of such a 'pre-contract' agreement (especially in a rising or vendor's market) is that it binds the vendor, preventing him or her from selling to someone else. The disadvantage is that your lawyer will not have had sufficient, probably not any, opportunity to carry out pre-contract enquiries. You are in effect being asked to sign with little knowledge of the vendor, or of the property,

You should not sign anything before speaking to your lawyer, who, it is hoped, you have already instructed prior to carrying out your serious searches for a property. If you are anxious to secure an agreement without delay, it may be possible to agree some conditions in the pre-contract, to provide you with some escape clauses, for example in relation to the presence, or future granting, of planning permission. Do not rush in. Speak to your lawyer first.

Declaring at an undervalue

You may be asked to declare property at an undervalue and pay a proportion of the purchase price 'under the table'. This will reduce the tax you pay on your purchase and the vendor's potential liability to tax on his or her capital gain. This practice, though illegal, has been very widespread.

The drawbacks to this are that, when you come to sell the property, unless you adopt the same procedure (by which time the authorities may well have clamped down further on the practice), you will have a larger capital gain and a higher tax bill. Moreover, if the matter should come to the knowledge of the authorities, they can (and do) have the property valued. You will then be charged any additional tax plus interest. If the underdeclaration is more than 12,000 euros and 20 per cent, then both vendor and purchaser can face substantial penalties under the 1989 *Ley de Tasas* (the law of public fees). Furthermore, if the local authority decides to purchase your property as part of a local development plan, you may find the price based on the price you paid (the underdeclared price). Lastly, if you decide to adopt the same practice on selling the property, do not assume that you will be paid the additional (under the table) sum by the purchaser.

The increasing tendency is to declare the correct sale price.

Purchasing at auction

As in the UK, the best-value properties are often those sold at auction by banks that have repossessed, or by other creditors seeking to recover outstanding debts, or where there is a dispute as to inheritance, or where the owner has died without heirs and the property needs to be sold. Auctions ordered by the courts, *subastos*, offer an opportunity to purchase property at sometimes a mere fraction of its market value, as the court is required to accept the highest offer, however low.

It is essential to inspect the property prior to bidding or, alternatively, arrange for a local estate agent (for a modest fee) to visit the property and provide you with a description and some photographs. Purchasing at auction can become expensive if you have to make several bid attempts before you are successful, especially if you obtain a report from a surveyor or other expert on each occasion. While your attendance at an auction is not necessary, it is an experience that you may not wish to miss.

Viewing the property

It is essential that you view the property several times, including in good and bad weather, and during the hours of darkness. Take care to listen to what noise is likely to affect you. Approach the property from different routes and consider how visitors might approach it. You might not appreciate them remembering that to reach you they have to turn left past the sewage works, continue on past the funeral director or climb the hill past the refuse dump.

You should not be deterred from returning to the property before deciding whether or not to proceed. If possible, try to ascertain why the owners wish to sell and how long (and it may be a question of years, rather than months) the property has been on the market. It may help to remember that the estate agent will receive commission several times the percentage of a UK colleague, albeit generally on a lower-price ticket, and ought to be prepared to answer your questions and arrange your various visits to the property.

Consider the property's location in relation to access to public transport and proximity to shops – chemists and so on. Look carefully not only at the building, but also at the garden and the neighbouring properties. Are the boundaries clearly marked? Is there any reason to suspect that other people have a right of way over the property? What about that well-worn path running through part of the property? Is there a well? Having a well in your garden may appear like an attractive feature. However, it is clearly not so desirable if you are sunning yourself in a state of semi-undress when you look up to see your neighbours or other inhabitants of the village walking through your garden to exercise their right to draw water from your well. If there is a well, or some other feature of the property that concerns you, speak to the agent and vendor, then raise it with your lawyer. Check also that the light switches work, there is hot and cold running water and that the toilet bowls are not cracked.

Whether you are buying an established property, a new one from a developer or purchasing a building plot, you should pay particular attention to the terrain. Attempt to ascertain whether the land is likely to flood. A stream or river may be picturesque during the summer months, but may overflow its banks during heavy autumn rains, making your garden unusable even if your house remains untouched. Fortunately, some areas that are prone to dampness and flooding are easily identified by their names. When considering buying a property always check in a dictionary the name of the road or area in case it has a negative meaning.

Whether you are buying property or land, a surveyor can advise you whether the land was or is suitable to build on, especially if he or she is familiar with the locality. Be alert also to the possibility that the land has been used as a dumping ground for refuse or chemical waste – if you are being offered what seems like a bargain, this may be the explanation.

It is wise to visit the local Council to ascertain what improvements are planned in the locality, including any airports, motorways and railway lines. Ask what planning permissions, if any, have been granted for neighbouring properties. Check whether or not the area is subject to flooding.

It is also sensible to check the size of the flat or building. Agents' details have been known to overestimate these, and a shortfall may give you an extra tool with which to negotiate on price. If you are buying a property in the countryside, the *catastral* description (see definition under What your lawyer should do) is likely to be vague, and you may wish to have the property measured by an official surveyor, whose charges for this are likely to be between 400 and 800 euros.

Surveyor's report

In the UK, almost all lending institutions insist on a basic structural survey before agreeing to grant a mortgage. Any self-respecting solicitor will advise a client to have a survey carried out prior to committing him- or herself to a purchase. A structural survey has two very important advantages. First, it prevents you from purchasing a property that is structurally unsound, perhaps dangerous, expensive to restore and perhaps difficult to dispose of. It should identify any woodworm and any movement in the property (which may have caused extensive damage to underground drainage channels or undermined the stability of the property). Second, a good report, even a basic one, often identifies non-structural defects – often minor, sometimes more significant. These may not deter you from your intended purchase, but give you ammunition to negotiate on the purchase price.

In Spain, the practice is very different. Spanish banks and, indeed, most UK financial institutions in Spain, only require a valuation of the property, which is carried out by a valuer, not a surveyor. This is clearly a sensible way to proceed if you are purchasing a tumbledown cottage that requires extensive renovation and where you are essentially paying for the plot of land. Equally, if you are an experienced builder with a portfolio of properties that you are seeking to renovate and sell on, taking the risk of not obtaining a structural survey would be entirely rational. In my opinion, for the individual purchaser who is investing significant capital (including much higher acquisition costs than in the UK) or taking on the liability of a mortgage, a decision to proceed without a survey is sheer folly. Why do it in Spain, where building standards are, if anything, lower than in the UK, when you would not do it at home?

A full structural survey can be expensive, from 800 euros to about 2,500 euros. You will also need to have it translated. Translators should translate into their mother tongue, so you should instruct an English speaker to do this. Remember, this expenditure may help you to negotiate a lower price and save you from taking on an expensive liability that will be difficult to offload. The estate agents, your lawyer and your lending institution should be able to advise of the names of suitable experts. There are expatriate surveyors (as well as architects and builders) who are now living and working in Spain. Some of the consulates keep lists of such professionals.

Whoever you instruct to inspect the property, ensure that a written report is provided and make it clear what is to be covered – that is, structural condition of roof, walls, foundations, all woodwork, drains' connections with mains or the septic tank, plumbing, electrical and heating installations.

What your lawyer should do

The essential preliminary enquiries that should be carried out before you commit yourself to the purchase are as follows.

1. Establish the vendor's title to the property. Is the person seeking to sell the property to you the true and complete owner of the property? The only reliable way of ascertaining this is to obtain a certificate from the Property Register (*Registro de la Propiedad*), at a cost of about 40 euros plus VAT. Too frequently reliance is placed on the cheaper *nota simple* but this does not carry with it the Register's guarantee of accuracy. A *nota simple* will be required, but only just prior to completion of the transfer to you. Similarly, vendors may show you a copy of the *escritura publica* that they were given when they purchased the property. This is a title deed to the property, and will also record the charges against the property. However, this *escritura publica* is not up to date, and will not show debts subsequently recorded against the property.

   One problem that can quite often occur is where a property is registered in joint names, and one of the owners, often a spouse, has died. Frequently the deceased will have left his or her share in the property to the surviving spouse, or other joint owner, by will. However, the will is insufficient to permit the passing of the property to a purchaser, and the property must first be transferred into the sole name of the surviving spouse.

2. Carry out an investigation into debts owed by the vendor which may attach to the property. In Spain there is a range of debts that can be registered against a property, and that attach to the property, rendering any unsuspecting purchaser liable to repay them. Your lawyer should check with the *Hacienda* (tax office), that there are no unpaid taxes that are likely to be recorded against the property. For the same reason he or she should also check that the local annual property tax (*impuesto sobre bienes inmuebles* or IBI) has been paid. The vendor should be able to produce the receipt for the last three payments, though your lawyer should also check with the *Recaudación Provincial* (Provincial Rates Office).

3. Inspect the *Certificación Catastral*. This is similar to the old register of rateable values in the UK. It records an assessment of the value of the

property for the purposes of calculating the local property tax or *impuesto sobre buenos inmuebles* (IBI), not the market value (though the declared long-term intention is to bring the two into line). The value will appear on the receipt for the last payment of the IBI. Unlike the Property Register, which is concerned with ownership, the *Catastro* records the precise location, a physical description and the location of the boundaries of the property, and includes a plan or aerial photograph. The description of the property in the *Catastro* is more accurate than that in the Property Register, and in case of any discrepancy between the two, the version in the *Catastro* is normally to be preferred. When you receive a copy of this you should compare it to the description in the certificate from the Property Register, and in any copy of the *escritura* that you have been shown, but especially with the situation on the ground. If you have any concerns, raise these with your lawyer straight away. Ignore any comments from the vendor or estate agent that it is not necessary to obtain a *Certificado Catastral* – their sole objective is to push the sale through, and they will naturally not welcome any delays caused by the 6–8 weeks that may be necessary to obtain the certificate;

4. Inspect the *plan parcial*. This is a plan of the plots of land that is drawn up for each *urbanismo* when it is registered with the local town planning department (*urbanismo del Ayuntamiento*). Your lawyer will want to confirm that the *urbanismo* has been authorized and is properly registered – there have been numerous instances of illegal developments, where purchasers have been left with having to settle the developers' debts, and/or have faced major problems in having local services extended to their estate.

5. Carry out a search at the local town planning department to ascertain whether there are any significant new developments in the pipeline that might affect your property. A town's urban plan is called the *Plan General de Ordenación Urbana*, usually abbreviated to the PGOU.

6. Check that the property complies with the 1988 *Ley de Costas*, or coastal law, under which there are likely to be restrictions in relation to buildings within 100 metres of the beach, and indeed perhaps as far as 1 kilometre inland.

7. For properties built within the last 10 years, or since 1988 in coastal areas, check that a building licence was granted and that a certificate of completion (*certificado de fin de obra*) and a licence of first occupation

(*licencia de primera ocupación*) were granted. Your vendor should have these, failing which copies can be obtained by your lawyer from the local council. If this licence and certificate were not issued, then you could face significant problems and in the worst case you could be ordered to demolish the property.

8. If you are purchasing an apartment or a property in an urbanization, ask to see proof of payment of charges levied by the Community of Property Owners (that is the body responsible for managing the development, in particular the common parts), and inspect the rules governing the Community and the minutes of its last meeting. For further details see Chapter 7. Your lawyer should ascertain whether there are any items of major expenditure planned for the foreseeable future. If you have a pet you will also need to know whether pets are permitted.

9. Inspect the owner's receipts for payment of utility bills. While these remain solely the liability of the person who signed the agreement with the utility company, it avoids having the services to the property cut off. If that were to happen, however, you simply pay a modest fee for reconnection, which in fact is no higher than the charge for changing the services into your own name.

10. Ascertain the catastral value of the property when the vendor purchased, in order to calculate the *plus valia* tax (the *arbitrio sobre el incremento del valos de los terrenos)*. This tax is payable by the vendor on the increase in the *catastral* value from the time of purchase to the sale. Although a liability of the vendor, sale contracts increasingly provide that this is to be paid by the purchaser. If this tax is to be paid by the vendor, but he or she fails to pay, the tax can still be levied against the property itself, despite the transfer to the purchaser. The *plus valia* tax should not be confused with the capital gains tax payable by a vendor on his or her true gain on the sale, and which remains normally payable by the vendor;

11. If the vendor is an offshore company, inspect receipts proving the payment of the annual 3 per cent tax.

12. If the property has been built within the last 10 years, obtain evidence of the builder's structural guarantee.

Once the preliminary enquiries have been completed, your survey has been carried out, and your finance confirmed, you should be in a position to proceed to sign the contract, the *contrato de compraventa.* This is normally drawn up by the vendor's estate agent, and your lawyer will need to consider with you whether there are any terms that you or he/she considers unacceptable. The contract must contain the names of the parties, a description of the property, a list of any items included or excluded from the sale, the price and how it is to be paid and the deposit. It should also record the completion date when all the parties are required to attend at the notary's office to sign the transfer of the property (*escritura*), how the balance of the purchase price is to be paid, and that the vendor gives vacant possession of the property. It should state who is to be responsible for the various expenses and taxes arising from the transaction.

In the past the vendor was responsible for the notary's fees, and the *plus valia* tax (*impuesto sobre el incremento del valor de los Terrenos* or IVT) arising from the increase in the catastral value of the property since he or she purchased it. The purchaser's obligations consisted of paying the transfer tax (*impuesto de transmisiones Patrimoniales*) and the fee for registering the transfer. The estate agents' fees are already included in the price, and accordingly are paid from the proceeds of sale.

Today contracts usually state that the purchaser is to pay all the costs and taxes (*todos los gastos*) arising out of the sale. This includes the *plus valia* and the notary's fees. You are unlikely to persuade the vendor to alter these terms, but you should seek a reduction in the price of the property, given that the vendor will not be meeting these expenses.

The deposit should be paid preferably to your lawyer, failing which to an estate agent with a bonded client account, never to any other agent and never to the vendor direct. The contract should provide that if the purchaser does not complete on the stated date he or she will lose the deposit. Similarly if the vendor does not complete the sale on that date, he or she will be required to pay a penalty to the purchaser equal to twice the deposit paid by the purchaser.

The contract should also contain a warranty from the vendor that he or she has disclosed all charges on the property. The warranty should provide that the vendor will pay all charges up until the date of sale, and that he or she will supply proof of up-to-date payment of all charges when attending the notary's office to execute the *escritura* on the date of completion. The vendor is also required to disclose whether or not he or she is resident in Spain and supply either his or her fiscal number if resident, or non-resident number. If the vendor is non-resident, the law requires the purchaser to retain 5 per cent of the declared purchase price and pay this to the *Hacienda*, as a guarantee that the non-resident vendor will meet his or her tax liabilities, including Spanish capital gains tax, and annual wealth tax. You will need to provide proof to the notary that you have paid this sum to the *Hacienda.*

Lastly, the contract should contain a warranty by the vendor that all the appropriate building and other licences have been granted.

While the signing of the *contrato de compraventa* creates a binding agreement, this is not sufficient to register the transfer in the Property Register. It is first necessary to transfer this private contract into a public deed by the execution by both parties of a conveyance, or *escritura de compraventa*, at the notary's office.

Just prior to the execution of the *escritura de compraventa*, your lawyer will need to request a *nota simple* from the land registry. This sets out information relating to the most recent charges or debts recorded against the property, and is required to verify that there have been no late charges against the property register prior to completion.

All the owners of the property, and if it is being purchased in joint names, all the purchasers, must attend for the execution of the *escritura*. So too must a representative of any lender. If someone is unable to attend he or she must execute a power of attorney (*poder*) to authorize someone else to attend on his or her behalf.

Once the *escritura de compraventa* has been executed, the notary should then proceed to register it in the Property Register, thereby creating a *escritura publica*. Registration of the transfer is not compulsory, and some people choose not to do so in order to avoid paying the transfer tax of 6 or 7 per cent and the stamp duty of 0.5 per cent (1 per cent in Andalusia). You should register. Firstly, if you do not, you will find it more difficult to sell your property. Secondly, you risk having charges registered against the property that will take precedence over your interest. These may be debts contracted by the vendor. Alternatively the vendor could fraudulently sell his or her property to an innocent third party who might register his or her interest before yours, and hence take precedence over you. Accordingly the registration should proceed as soon as possible. To register your lawyer will need to send to the Property Registry not only the *escritura,* but also the receipts proving payment of the various taxes. This can take some time. Accordingly, a special notification should be sent by fax from the notary's office on the day of completion. This will guarantee that no one else can register the property while the notary obtains the receipts.

It usually takes about two to three months after completion for the *escritura* to be registered. The *escritura compraventa* is stamped by the Property Register, thereby becoming an *escritura publica*, and returned to the notary, who should provide you with an authorized copy. The notary keeps the original.

The costs of purchase

It is difficult to give a precise estimate of the total costs and taxes involved in a transaction, not least because nowadays it is common for the purchaser to pay the vendor's *plus valia* tax on the increase in the catastral value of the property since he or she bought it. As a guide, costs will total around 10–15 per cent of the purchase price, but if you are lucky the total may fall just below 10 per cent. The individual items are as follows.

▪ The lender's arrangement fee (about 1 per cent), plus a valuation fee of around 1 per cent.

▪ Your surveyor's fee of 800–2,500 euros.

▪ The transfer tax or *Impuesto de Transmisiones Patrimoniales*. This is 7 per cent of the declared sale price in Andalusia, and 6 per cent elsewhere. There is no transfer tax on purchases from a developer, but instead you pay IVA (VAT) at 7 per cent.

▪ The fee for registration at the Property Register. This is likely to be about 500 euros.

▪ Stamp duty of 1 per cent in Andalusia, and 0.5 per cent elsewhere.

▪ The notary's fees. These are officially fixed, and the level is determined by the size of the property and the price. You will need to budget for 300–700 euros.

▪ The *plus valia* tax or the *arbitrio sobre el incremento del valor de los terrenos*, ie a tax on the increase in the official value (not the market value) of the *land* since it was last sold. If you are buying an apartment or a property with very little land, or one that was purchased by your vendor only recently, the tax is likely to be very modest. On the other hand, if you are purchasing a property with a substantial amount of land that has not changed hands for some years, the tax could be quite substantial. The rate of tax varies between 10 per cent and 40 per cent depending upon the time elapsed since the last sale, and the location of the property.

Note that the *plus valia* tax is distinct from the separate capital gains tax that a non-resident must pay on the profit from the sale of a property. The rates of the *plus valia* at the date of the vendor's purchase, and the current rate, can both be obtained from the local tax office.

▌ Your own lawyer's fees – approximately 1 per cent of the purchase price, plus VAT, plus the minor disbursements relating to the searches carried out.

Insurance

You need to ensure that you have insurance cover in place. In addition to Spanish insurance companies, there are a number of UK companies that will provide requisite cover. The advantage of insuring with a UK company is that the policy will be in English and any claim can be made in English.

Whatever policy you take out, ensure that you have sufficient cover. If you underinsure you will not be able to claim your full loss. Public liability insurance is cheap and, accordingly, a high level of cover (consider 1,500,000 euros) is worthwhile.

When you need to claim, ensure that you do so within the strict time limits and by recorded delivery. If you intend to occupy the property for only short periods or to let it out, you should inform your insurers.

5 Financing the purchase of your Spanish home

Taking out a mortgage is a serious and long-term commitment. For this reason many foreign residents prefer to deal with institutions where the documentation and discussions are in English. There are several banking institutions that provide these. Two of the most popular are Lloyds TSB and Barclays, with Web sites in English advising on the services they offer in Spain (see Appendix 1). There are no legal restrictions on the currency in which the mortgage is granted, and accordingly Lloyds TSB and Barclays can offer you a mortgage in sterling, thereby avoiding a fluctuating exchange rate causing alterations in your repayments.

In addition there are a number of German banks present in Spain, where staff generally speak English to a high level. There are also several Spanish banks well-accustomed to assisting foreign buyers, including *Banca March* which operates in the Balearic and Canary Islands. It also has offices in London, and will lend in sterling. The advantage of a Spanish loan in euros is that over the last few years Spain has had some of the lowest interest rates in Europe.

Mortgages can be obtained over 20 or even 30 years, and in some cases mortgages of 100 per cent of the value of the property are possible. In practice, however, most banks only lend up to 80 per cent of the value of the property, and of course the mortgage will not cover the substantial acquisition costs of a property in Spain. If you are non-resident, however, you may find difficulty obtaining a loan of more than 70 per cent. Spanish banks tend to offer shorter mortgage terms of 3–20 years for a resident and 3–10 years for a non-resident. UK lending institutions are more prepared to grant longer repayment terms.

All mortgage lenders in Spain go through a very similar procedure to that applicable in other countries. The bank will need to check your financial standing and will require details of residence status, employment position, income and tax status. If you are self-employed, you will be asked for your accounts and tax liabilities in the preceding three years. Arrangement fees vary, but start from about 400 euros, and are often based on a percentage of the property, frequently 1.5 per cent. It is worth shopping around.

In Spain, mortgage lenders do not require a survey of the property concerned, although some ask for a property valuation. The latter is merely designed to estimate the market value.

A valuation fee works out at about 1 per cent on a property valued in the region of 400,000 euros, is less for more expensive properties, and can go up to about 2 per cent, or even slightly more, for cheaper properties.

Before deciding on a mortgage lender, you should shop around the main institutions to consider the variations and any special promotions that they may be running. Ensure that you fully understand the policies on offer. Taking independent advice may well save you substantial financial loss, not to mention anxiety and heartache.

Once the lender has approved your application, you will be sent a mortgage offer. Most major institutions are willing to process applications prior to you locating a property to indicate how much they would be prepared to lend to you and on what terms.

One option is to raise the finance in the UK by using any UK property as security. The cheapest option may be to ask your existing mortgage lender if it would increase the mortgage facility, thereby avoiding legal fees, land registry fees and even an arrangement fee. You could also take the opportunity of considering re-mortgaging your UK property – you may succeed in reducing your existing repayments to offset partly the costs of financing your Spanish property.

The main drawback of borrowing in the UK is that interest rates have tended to be higher here than in Spain. On the other hand, if you are paying your repayments from funds in the UK, your repayments will not increase if the value of sterling falls.

If you are buying from a developer, you may find its terms for a loan more attractive than those of a bank mortgage. Do take legal advice before committing yourself, however. A particular point to watch out for is the consequences of late payment or missing a payment. It is vital that the agreement permits you to remedy this situation with only a modest penalty. Similarly you should ensure that you have the right to make early repayment (your future financial circumstances may make this a sensible course of action, or you may wish to sell before the end of the mortgage term). Developers' agreements sometimes require lenders to pay a penalty for early redemption of the loan, and this should be avoided.

There are a number of Spanish government schemes aimed at assisting the housing market. Collectively such housing is known as *Vivienda de Protección Oficial* or VPO. Several of these projects are specifically aimed at those on low incomes, but others consist of providing subsidized funding to developers. Foreigners are entitled to purchase properties in such developments, but even here prospective purchasers must be resident, and have an income of less than 1,500 euros. Only a modest down payment is required, though if you are able to make a greater initial investment this will reduce the interest rate on the remainder of the debt. Clearly, if you can invest a substantial amount of capital, this will have the effect of reducing your monthly expenditure, and may enable you to reduce the level of your income to bring you within the terms of the scheme. In practice such housing is unlikely to be a viable option for most foreigners contemplating purchasing property in Spain.

6 Buying a new property and having a property built

The details set out in Chapter 4 relating to the purchase of your property are of general application, and for the most part apply also to the purchase of a new property, and to having a property built.

If you are buying a new property, you may well have to buy it unseen ('off plan') and wait at least a year for it to be constructed. Buying a plot of land or having a house built for you is invariably much cheaper than buying a house built by a developer. Whether you are buying from a developer or purchasing a building plot, you should pay particular attention to the terrain and the matters set out in Chapter 4 under the heading Viewing the property.

Building plots

If you are building your own house, or having a house built, then it is imperative that you find yourself a good lawyer, and a good architect. You must also be prepared to devote a lot of time in personal supervision of the works, at least if you want the outcome to correspond to what you had in mind at the outset.

The land you buy may already form part of an urbanization with services already arranged and with the benefit of planning permission, or may be totally without services or any planning permission. In either case, give consideration to the nature of the underlying surface – it could have a major impact on the costs of construction. Granite, for example, is not susceptible to being broken up or hewn out, even with pneumatic tools – expensive explosives will be required. The key to ascertaining the nature of the land is to ask as many questions as you can, not merely from the vendor, but also of neighbours and at the local council. Above all, have an expert examine the land. In rural areas regulations frequently dictate that a building plot must be of a certain minimum size – 10,000 square metres is a common requirement, but it can be more, especially if the land has no source of water. Ensure that you buy enough land!

It is particularly important to take note of what you see on the ground. Be alert to any signs of a path running across the plot, which may be a right of way, and also to the boundaries. Check the description of the land in the *Catastro*, including the measurements and location of the boundaries. If the details in the *Catastro* do not correspond to what can be seen on the ground, then either the *Catastro* is incorrect, or the position on the ground may have been changed, and perhaps boundaries moved. It is important to ensure that the two correspond, and to apply to change the details on the *catastral* if they appear incorrect.

If you are having your own property built you are all the more in need of help and guidance from lawyers and other experts. If you are to carry out any of the enquiries or to make applications for planning permission, etc, yourself, you either need to speak Spanish fairly well, or you need assistance from someone who can. Obviously, help and guidance from someone who has already had their own home built, especially in the same locality, and who can come with you to the local council's *urbanissmo* or town planning department, can be invaluable. You also need to check on the building regulations which dictate such matters as how high you can build, how close to the boundary you can construct the house, the height of any boundary wall, etc.

In Spain land is zoned into different categories that govern the type of development permitted, including green and rural zones where building is extremely restricted. There are additional restrictions relating to development on the coast. If you are proposing to purchase land or a property in the country, such as a *finca* or farmhouse, your lawyer will need to verify whether it is in an area *urbano* or *rustico*. Building in the latter is not permitted, or when it is, is subject to substantial restrictions. Accordingly banks will only loan up to 50 per cent of the value of the property, and will only grant shorter mortgage terms of up to about 10 years. You or your lawyer will also need to ascertain the proportion of the plot which the property may occupy, and any restrictions on building, renovating or extending the property. In an area *urbano* you and your advisers will need to check the *Plan General de Ordenación Urbana* (PGOU). Remember, however, that this is subject to renewal every four years, and may be subject to imminent change. Purchasers of plots forming part of an urbanization need to inspect the *proyecto de urbanización*, the *plan parcial* showing their plot, and enquire as to what other planning permissions have been granted in the vicinity.

Remember that the information obtained prior to your purchase is merely a snap-shot of the situation at a particular time. If your property is in an area *urbano*, and there is land near to your property that has not been developed, it is very likely that it is only a matter of time before the land becomes yet another construction site on which a property will be built that may not be to your liking, and may effect your view and the value of your property. This is simply a risk you take, unless you purchase a remaining plot of land in an area already well developed.

The land may already have planning permission (*permiso de obra*). You will need to check carefully what is permitted, and any conditions attached to the permission. If there is no planning permission, you will need to factor the cost of obtaining this into your calculations – this can be up to 5 per cent of the total building costs. If you are concerned that there is a risk of planning permission being refused, and you are being pressed to commit yourself and do not want to risk this plot slipping through your fingers, ask your lawyer about having a condition in the contract that enables you to avoid the contract if an expert advises that the land will be expensive, difficult or impossible to build on.

A difficulty that frequently arises with land and property in the countryside is that ownership has never been registered, and accordingly there is no *escritura.* Your lawyer will need to be satisfied that the person purporting to the be the owner of the property does in fact have title. The vendor can establish that he or she does own the land using a procedure known as *expediente de dominio* which includes publication of details in the Spanish official gazette, the *Boletín Oficial de Estado.* Particular care is also required in these cases in relation to the investigation of any rights of way over the property, and in ascertaining the boundaries.

If the plot is not connected to the various services, you should check if there are likely to be any problems with connecting to the mains water and mains sewerage, gas, electricity and telephone networks. Even if these services extend to neighbouring properties, you will almost certainly bear the costs of connecting to the networks. Check on access to the property, including access for works vehicles that will need to deliver supplies or carry out works at the property during construction. Also, if the boundaries are not already fenced, the contract of sale is likely to require you to erect fencing at your expense.

Besides the option of instructing an architect to design a property, there are companies that offer a range of standard properties that they will construct for you and to which they will make internal modifications to suit your requirements. If this option appeals, ask to see examples of properties already constructed by the company. You need to be absolutely certain what is included in the price, in particular in relation to fittings in the kitchen and bathroom, as well as the garage and garden. This is obviously a cheaper option than the individually architect-designed route and, as the companies have often constructed their models with the approach of the local planning authorities in mind, you should be less likely to encounter problems from that quarter.

Employing an architect will obviously increase the costs of construction. He or she will normally prepare the (detailed) list of specifications (*memoria de calidades*). This will indicate the nature and quality (and hence cost) of the materials to be used in the construction of your house. You will obviously need to discuss this with the architect in some detail. The *memoria de calidades* will form the basis of any builder's bid to do the work. While it would be advisable to obtain several bids, your architect should be able to help you choose which builders to invite to bid, and which of the bids to accept.

Depending on the degree of his or her involvement, the architect's fees will be around 6 per cent of the total price of the house, with an additional 3 per cent being payable to the architectural engineer (*aparejador*), who oversees the progress of the construction and verifies that it complies with the various building regulations. He or she is also responsible for providing the confirmation necessary to obtain the Certificate of Completion (*Certificado de Fin de Obra)* and Licence for First Occupation (*Licencia de Primera Ocupación*). An architect normally requires 70 per cent of his or her fee when construction commences, with 30 per cent payable on completion.

The building contract

Whether you buy a property from a developer, purchase the land yourself and purchase a standard building package or instruct an architect and builder to design and build a house for you, the building contract should cover the following:

∎ the total cost, to include all necessary certificates and licences;
∎ a detailed description and plan of the property to be built;
∎ the quality of the materials to be used;
∎ a schedule of construction and ancillary work;
∎ the completion date and penalty clauses for late completion of the work (and late payment by yourself);
∎ the proportion of the costs of the *comunidad de proprietarios* for which you will be liable;
∎ insurance cover during the period of construction;
∎ that the developer will pay all debts and expenses associated with the land until the property is transferred to you;
∎ the bank guarantee in relation to the return of advance payments should the construction not be completed;
∎ the deposit (usually 10–15 per cent of the total cost) and stage payments, normally a further 15–25 per cent on completion of the roof, 15–25 per cent when the property is fully fitted out, and the remainder on signing of the *escritura*;
∎ (ideally) a term stating that a percentage (say 5 per cent) of the contract price should be withheld for several months as a guarantee should any problems appear.

Once the building work is finished, you must take a careful look at the contract to ensure that every detail is covered, from doors and windows, to kitchen, bathroom and toilet fittings, to wall and floor finishes.

Do not be surprised if the work takes longer than envisaged. The developer is bound to hit some problem or other and is allowed some leeway to complete the task. Do visit the construction site from time to time to satisfy yourself that matters are proceeding properly and raise any concerns that you have. An error in the construction can be much more easily and speedily corrected if identified at an early stage.

Buying from a developer

Many new properties are sold by developers prior to construction, although you may be able to inspect a show house. A reputable developer may well have sold the entire stock before work has even commenced. Purchasers buy on the basis of plans. Indeed, in the most popular areas, you should be suspicious if a development is nearly completed and a number of properties remain unsold. This may be an indication that the developer is overcharging, that there is something else wrong with the development or that it is the developer that is putting others off.

You or your lawyer should check on the financial health of the developer and on the insurance cover and the bank guarantee. The latter is important to ensure the return of the advance payments you will make, should the builder go into liquidation, or otherwise fail to complete the building. Builders are required by Spanish law to provide such guarantees, and indeed the law also requires that the purchaser receive interest at 6 per cent per annum on the sums he or she paid out.

If you are intending to buy from one of the UK companies operating in Spain, you should proceed with the same caution. The builder has probably set up a Spanish company and will probably seek to avoid using the financial strength of the UK business to bail out the Spanish subsidiary should it run into difficulties.

There are various advantages in purchasing a new property – you obtain a bright new and clean property of which you are the first occupier, and the likelihood is that it will have double glazing, up-to-date insulation, central heating, good ventilation and good security. If you are one of the early purchasers on the development, you will have considerable freedom in choosing the precise location of your house or apartment. In addition, you avoid the expense and inconvenience of renovation works, yet have the freedom to choose your own colour schemes and materials, as well as the ability to agree some variations.

In the case of purchases from a developer, the total price is fixed at the outset. Many developments consist of a complex with various sports and other facilities, including a swimming pool. A major disadvantage is that you might be paying for the property for a considerable period of time while still having to finance your existing accommodation.

A major difference between Spain and the UK in this process is that in Spain the builder remains the owner until completion of the property. The sale and transfer of the property to you must wait until the certificate of completion of works, and the licence of first occupation have been granted. Only then can the *escritura* be executed. The main practical difficulty that this causes is that you have no security to offer potential lenders, and accordingly you cannot obtain a mortgage to finance the advance payments (*pagos adelantados*) that you will need to pay to the builder.

Once the property is completed, however, you will probably have the option of taking over the proportion of the developer's mortgage of the development that relates to your property. The advantages of doing this, rather than taking out your own mortgage, are that you will not have to pay a property valuation fee, you may avoid stamp duty, and the costs of instructing the notary and registering the property are much less. Generally the proportion of the value of the property that you can mortgage in this way is limited to 60 per cent. If you require a greater level of finance you will have to take out a second mortgage to cover the balance, and accordingly it may not be worth your while taking over the developer's mortgage.

After completion of the work, you and a representative of the developer should meet together to ensure that you are happy with the work that has been carried out. I strongly recommend that you instruct a surveyor or architect to inspect the property on your behalf at this point. It is the occasion when a record is made as to whether or not you accept the work and, if you accept it, whether this is with or without any reservations. If the property does not correspond to your expectations as set out in the contract, then a list should be recorded (a snag list) of what is missing or faulty.

Once your property is completed you will need to make a declaration of new work, *a declaración de la obra nueva*, to the *catastro*, which costs 0.5 per cent of the declared value of the construction, and register it on the Property Register. To make the declaration and to register your house, you will need the *certificado final de obra*, the *licencia de obra* and the *licencia de primera ocupación.*

The guarantees

A builder is by law (*Ley de Ordenación de Edificación 1999*) required to provide three guarantees, as follows:

▐ a 10-year guarantee in relation to the foundations, load-bearing walls and other structural parts. A builder must have an insurance policy to cover this. The policy must be handed to the notary, who must record the details on the *escritura* in order for registration of your title to take place;

▐ a 3-year guarantee in relation to damage caused by defective construction materials, and matters which render the property uninhabitable;

▐ a one-year guarantee covering minor defects, such as decoration and other finishes.

Buying an apartment or private property on a housing development

Most foreign property owners of Spanish properties have bought apartments, or houses in urbanizations. In an apartment block, or urbanization, each proprietor owns the private parts of his or her apartment or house, but the common parts including lifts, hallways and stairs, the entranceway to the building, the approach road, gardens, pathways and so on are owned by the *Comunidad de Propietarios*, or Community of Owners. The powers, rights and responsibilities of the *Comunidad* and the rules governing its relationship with proprietors, are increasingly subject to the Law of Horizontal Property. This law dates from 1960, but was substantially changed in 1999, extending the range of properties covered by the legislation, and introducing measures to improve the running of a *Comunidad,* and making it easier for the *Comunidad* to recover debts owed to it by its members.

These properties are often more affordable and offer owners a number of advantages, including often a higher level of security, easy maintenance and less responsibility than if they owned a separate dwelling. Developments frequently have facilities such as pools and gardens that you can enjoy without the inconvenience and burden of the extra maintenance required.

On the other hand, you have less privacy, are more at risk from disturbance by your neighbours and can be subject to large service charges/community fees over which you have little control. In some instances, factions can develop within the *Comunidad,* with deep animosity between owners, and arguments erupting about every conceivable detail of how the development should be run.

In holiday resorts, you may find that the communal swimming pool or sports facilities are so overloaded as to be of no benefit. Accordingly, if you are purchasing a resale as opposed to a new property, you would do well to make your initial visit during the peak season and ask what restrictions are placed on the use of such facilities.

Before agreeing to buy such an apartment or home, it is imperative that you ask to see the rules governing the *Comunidad*. These set out the rights and obligations of proprietors and the rules for the smooth functioning of the development. They will govern what you can and cannot do. They may prohibit you from exercising any business or profession; impose restrictions on renting; prohibit the keeping of pets; or impose a uniform colour scheme on awnings and restrict external alterations to your property. These rules also set out what is covered by the service charges and how the cost of these is to be divided.

In most cases, the everyday management of the development is carried out by a small committee, often assisted by an unelected paid administrator, but subject to overall control by of all the property owners. A general assembly convenes once a year and on other occasions if necessary. Votes are by simple majority on most issues, though in relation to a change in the Community's charter, or to major modifications to the structure of an apartment block, the Law of Horizontal Property requires a unanimous vote. On other issues a three-fifths majority may be required, and in relation to some matters those who have not protested against a proposed course of action, and do not attend the meeting, will be counted as being in favour! Proprietors can attend by proxy if they are unable to attend in person. Voting rights are weighted according to the size of your property, with voting rights of owners of larger properties carrying greater weight.

You should ask to see the minutes of the last two or three Annual General Meetings to see what issues were discussed. This should give you an idea of any problems associated with the development, and of any significant expenditure that is on the horizon.

You should also see the receipts for the last two or three years' services charges, or Community fees (*cuota*). You need to see these, not only to ensure that they have been paid by the vendor, but also because they will give you an idea of the charges that you will have to pay if you purchase. The charges include the costs of maintaining, repairing, cleaning, lighting, heating and insuring the common parts and the administration involved for the development. All proprietors have to pay a share of these costs in accordance with the proportionate value or size of their property, and irrespective of whether or not they make use of the facilities. There is no rebate if your property is unoccupied for prolonged periods of time, so take care if you are looking for a holiday apartment. Note that garage and parking facilities often have to be purchased separately.

You would be especially well advised when considering the purchase of such a property to introduce yourself to neighbours if the opportunity arises or can be created. A very short conversation may immediately warn you off, and a longer conversation may reveal problems with the management of the development that at least require questions to be asked by you and/or your lawyer. Ask them bluntly 'Would you buy again?'!

Look carefully at the condition of the development. Are any major expenses likely to be required in the near future? Ask your lawyer to ask the vendor whether he or she knows of any impending expenditure. The Law of Horizontal Property, however, requires the maintenance of a reserve fund amounting to at least 5 per cent of the normal operating budget of the *Comunidad*, though this only provides limited protection.

If another proprietor is rowdy or endangers the health and safety of the block or development or other proprietors, the *Comunidad* can take court action to obtain an injunction ordering the offender to desist, and also obtain an award of compensation for the breaches that have been committed. If the culprit fails to comply with a court injunction, he or she can be held in contempt of court and the court can expel him or her from the property for up to three years. A tenant can be evicted immediately, even if he or she has a rental contract that is still running.

Once you have purchased, ensure that you give the *Comunidad* an address in Spain where you can receive any legal notices. If you fail to do this, the *Comunidad* will write to you at the property itself, or in certain circumstances leave a notice on the communal notice board.

8 Heating and utility bills

Choosing how to heat your home

Heating requirements vary greatly according to the location of your home, its type, size and insulation, whether you live at the property throughout the year and whether it is occupied during the day. In northern Spain the climate is wet and often as cold as in the UK. Central Spain can be colder. Even slightly inland on the Costa del Sol you will definitely need heating in the winter months.

One disadvantage with many Spanish homes is that they are designed to remain cool during the hot summer season. In cold periods their tiled floors and concrete walls make your home seem particularly cold. In most Spanish homes you will need some form of heating facility. In deciding how to heat your home you also have to consider the present heating system in the property, the costs of installing a new system, the life expectancy of a new system and your estimated consumption. In apartment blocks there is frequently a central gas-fired under-floor heating system, which is paid in whole or in part through your community fees.

Electricity

Electricity is a convenient form of heating, especially for smaller flats and coastal properties in the south where your heating requirements will be modest. It has the great advantage of being easy and inexpensive to install, so it is often the choice of landlords. The disadvantage of electricity, however, is that the running costs are high.

Gas

The advantages of gas are that it is clean and relatively economical. However, for the most part only properties in the main towns and larger cities are connected to the gas mains. Elsewhere, bottled butane gas is commonly used. This is relatively economic, and in most areas bottled butane can be delivered to your home. Canisters of 23.5 kilograms cost about 10 euros, with a deposit for the bottle of about 20 euros. You should keep a spare full bottle, as it is difficult to determine when a bottle is likely to run out.

One disadvantage of gas is that it can be dangerous if any gas-run apparatus is not functioning properly. Accordingly a word of caution is appropriate: beware carbon monoxide poisoning. It is likely that the problem is, in fact, quite widespread, with many people being unaware of their exposure and the cause of symptoms they are suffering. Symptoms resemble those associated with flu – headache, fatigue, nausea and problems with vision and hearing.

Carbon monoxide is a colourless, odourless gas, associated with gas and also oil, wood and coal-burning appliances. Almost invariably, the problem arises from a faulty or incorrectly used appliance. Appliances should be regularly serviced and replaced when appropriate. A faulty appliance is not only dangerous, but is inefficient and accordingly more expensive to run.

Solar energy

Solar energy is renewable, clean, silent and free. Moreover, a system that uses solar energy requires very little maintenance and should last 20 or 30 years. Solar energy is particularly popular for heating water in Austria and Germany. Spain has rather more hours of sunshine and so solar energy is capable of meeting the majority of your needs for heating both your rooms and your water. A major disadvantage is the relatively high instal-lation cost. A second drawback is that you will need a back-up system (although portable electric radiators may suffice).

Air-conditioning

Increasingly modern buildings have the benefit of air-conditioning, a great relief during the height of summer. If the property is without this facility, it may be worthwhile obtaining an estimate, especially if you are purchasing a new home. Note that for older people, some form of system for lowering the temperature is likely to be essential, and if there is no central air conditioning, serious consideration should be given to obtaining a portable gas cooler.

Electricity bills

Electricity bills are issued every two months in Spain, rather than quarterly. Your bill will consist of a subscription for the service paid in advance, plus an amount depending on the quantity of electricity consumed. Electricity supplied is at 220 volts, which is compatible with 240-volt appliances purchased in the UK, but not with equipment purchased in the United States. If you are proposing to purchase an old property, you will need to check the voltage, as it may be wired for the older 110-volt system formerly in use.

When registering with the electricity company you must decide first the level of kilowatt-hours (kWh) of your electricity supply. This will determine the tariff applicable to your supply. The wattage you require can range from as little as 3 kWh if your needs are limited to lighting and running such electrical appliances as a television, refrigerator and vacuum cleaner. If you wish to be able to run a washing machine, dishwasher and electric cooker, you will probably need a supply between 9 and 18 kWh – the latter being probably the most popular choice for a family. For homes with numerous electrical appliances likely to be switched on at the same time or with an electric system for heating rooms or water, you should discuss your needs with a representative of the electricity company.

The appliances that place the greatest demands in kilowatts on your system are as follows (figures indicate the maximum the appliances would use):

- water heater – 4,500;
- cooker's hotplates – 4,000;

- dishwasher – 3,000;
- washing machine – 3,000;
- tumble-dryer – 3,000;
- electric kettle – 1,800;
- oven – 1,200;
- iron – 1,100;
- hair-dryer – 1,100.

Accordingly, a family household in which a water heater, kettle, washing machine, oven and hairdryer could well be operated simultaneously would require up to 11.6 kilowatts without taking into account the less hungry items, such as lighting, televisions, computers, fridge, freezer and so on.

Water bills

While water is in plentiful supply in the north of the country, the hottest and most popular tourist areas suffer from often severe water shortages. In rural areas *fincas* may be some distance from the mains supply, and so have to be supplied from tankers, causing an added expense. If the property boasts a well in the garden, you will need to check whether others have rights to use it, and also the quality of the water and whether it dries up during the summer.

For the most part mains water supplies in Spain are metered. Prices vary according to the region, but bills can be quite hefty. An average family can easily use about 500 litres of water per day. About 60 per cent of an average family's consumption relates to the taking of baths and showers and the flushing of the toilet. Accordingly, substantial reductions in consumption can be made by taking showers instead of baths and choosing the toilet cistern carefully – more modern cisterns use a third or less of the amount used by older toilets. Always check where the main stop-valve or stopcock is located in case you need to turn off the water supply in an emergency.

The telephone

To have a line installed you will need to visit your local office of Telefonica. You can find out the address by telephoning 1004, and if you wish can start your application over the telephone. To subscribe you will need to show your residence card or passport, proof of residence such as a recent utility bill, and your *escritura*, or rental contract if your home is rented. Information about Telefonica is available on its Web site: www.telefonica.es

Direct debit

There is much to be said for paying by direct debit, particularly if you are away from the property for extended periods.

Settling in

The New Spain

In the last 40 years Spain has undergone a transformation. In the early 1960s Spain was a poor country with a mostly peasant population. With intensive foreign investment and membership of the European Community, the last 20 years especially has seen rapid economic growth. Spain is now wealthy. It boasts a substantial industrial sector (it is one of the world's largest car producers) as well as healthy agricultural and tourist industries, and has one of the highest standards of living in the world.

The tourist industry has continued to grow, with over 50 million visitors to Spain each year. The market has changed, in that many of those coming to the Iberian peninsula are not looking for the package holiday of sand and sun, but are increasingly visiting cultural and historic sites, inland Spain and the northern coast. Much of the agricultural sector has changed out of all recognition, with acres of land now devoted to the mass production of fruit and vegetables for the north-European market, most striking in the endless stretches of plastic sheeting on the Costa de Almería.

With increasing prosperity has come improved education at all levels, a shift away from traditional values and horizons in favour of greater individuality and freedom of expression. The last 20 years have also seen the availability of divorce (illegal until 1981), increasing participation of women in the labour market and in decision making, one of the lowest birth rates in the industrialized world, and accordingly far smaller families than previously.

Spain has also undergone tremendous political changes since the death of Franco in 1975. The return of the monarchy in the form of King Juan Carlos was accompanied by the creation of a new constitution based on compromise, the right to form trade unions, the election of a democratic government, entry into the European Community and in 1982 membership of NATO. King Juan Carlos and the royal family have proved extremely adept at winning the confidence of the nation, and the monarchy is very popular.

The *gestor*

One aspect of life in Spain that is only just beginning to change is the seemingly limitless enthusiasm of Spanish government agencies for generating paperwork, and creating every conceivable kind of hurdle to undermine the smooth running of their daily contact with the public. Procedures which in other countries can be carried out speedily, or by post, or by telephone or over the Internet require a personal attendance, often necessitating a return journey of several hours, followed by hours of queuing at different counters, usually at opposite ends of the official building.

Help is at hand, however. To deal with this nightmare of administrative bureaucracy the Spaniards have created the profession of *gestor*. Licensed to advise and represent Spaniards and foreigners, he or she can greatly ease the burden of your everyday dealings with the state. The *gestor* can provide you with invaluable advice, or better still can handle these procedures on your behalf. His or her fee is modest. After you have spent several days pulling your hair out, you will wonder why you did not use his or her services in the first place, and spend your time in some more worthwhile pursuit. While initially you may wish to rely on your lawyer for matters relating to your purchase, you should make enquiries amongst the expatriate community and any Spanish friends as to any *gestors* they would recommend.

Your right to stay in Spain

Citizens of the European Union are entitled to live and work in any of the member states. No special documentation is required for your first 90 days.

As of 1 March 2003, certain categories of citizens of the European Union who wish to stay in Spain for more than 90 days do *not* need to apply for a residence card. These new regulations cover employees, the self-employed, students, and dependants of EU nationals who are themselves EU nationals. This exemption does not apply to the majority of EU citizens who have retired or who have independent means, and who must accordingly still apply for a residence card. Those who are not required to obtain a residence card may still do so if they wish to have proof of their residence status.

Applications for a residence permit are made to the local *Comisaria de Policia* or to the *Oficina de Extranjeros.* You should take with you a full valid passport, and three passport-sized photographs. If you are retired, or not otherwise earning an income, you will need to produce evidence that you have the resources to support yourself. Proving that you have a level of income equivalent to the Spanish retirement pension, for example by producing past bank statements, is sufficient. You will also need to produce evidence of health insurance or registration with the Spanish state system. Students need to prove that they are enrolled in a recognized educational establishment. For children and other dependants you will need their birth certificates.

It is advisable to carry your residence permit with you at all times as it is a form of identification and can also be requested at any time by a police officer. The card entitles you to travel to any part of Spain, including the Canary Islands and the Balearic Islands. On the card you will find your NIE (Foreigner Identification Number). This your tax number.

Further information on residence permits is available on www.mir.es, the Web site of the Ministry of the Interior.

Retiring to Spain

Spain is a popular location for people who are retired or planning their retirement. It is hardly a surprising choice compared to retiring in the UK, given the weather in most regions, and the lower housing costs. In most cases, the sale of your UK home will enable you to buy a very comfortable home in Spain and still have a substantial surplus.

It is important, however, to be realistic, for it is retired expatriates who are the most likely to return home. Consider what you are likely to miss in the UK, if you are likely to feel at home in Spain, how you will manage with the Spanish language and how you will cope with advancing age and possible illness and the loss of a partner.

If, after considering these things, you are determined to make the move, there are several areas, in particular in parts of the Costa del Sol, where much of what you may miss about life in the UK is duplicated, including cricket, the great British pub, British food and Anglican church services. Details of what is available in each region are set out in Chapter 2. The most popular areas tend to be the most expensive, but you may find them more conducive to making a home and developing a feeling of belonging.

There is no problem with receiving UK state and private pensions in Spain. As a retired person, you are entitled to use the Spanish health system on the same basis as a Spanish citizen. One matter that you do need to consider is exchange rate fluctuations. The problem will, of course, disappear when the UK eventually adopts the euro. In the meantime, you could move some of your investments to Spain. Alternatively, you could just accept that there is a risk that sterling may suffer modest falls in value, and discuss with your financial adviser how quickly you could move your investments if it was felt that sterling was likely to become particularly weak. Issues relating to inheritance are covered in Chapter 13. Advice to pensioners is available from various organizations, including Help the Aged.

Payment of other UK benefits while living in Spain

The principle of free movement of labour within the European Union requires that citizens of member states should not be impeded from living and working in other member states. Accordingly, citizens of EU countries should not lose any of their rights to welfare benefits by moving to Spain. Those currently in receipt of an old-age pension, invalidity and disability benefits, widows' benefits or benefits received as a result of an accident at work, or an occupational disease, are entitled to have their benefits paid to them irrespective of where they choose to live. The relevant benefits should be paid gross and include any increases. Incapacity benefit will only be paid to those who have paid Class 1 or Class 2 and 4 National Insurance contributions.

If you have not yet retired, your existing entitlement to a UK pension will be frozen and you will receive a reduced pension from the UK authorities when you reach retirement age. For those approaching retirement, it may be worthwhile making voluntary payments to bring your National Insurance contributions up to the level entitling you to a full pension. You should contact The Pension Service's International Pension Centre (part of the Department for Work and Pensions, a renamed part of the former DSS, on tel: 0191 218 7777) and the Inland Revenue's Centre for Non-Residents (tel: 0845 070 0040), to ask for up-to-date information and advice, including whether you should pay Class 2 or Class 3 contributions. The former is the more expensive option but entitles you to incapacity benefit.

As to unemployment benefit, those out of work are entitled to have the Jobseeker's Allowance paid to them in Spain for up to 13 weeks. You must have been registered as a job seeker for at least four weeks before you left the UK, and have been available for work up until your departure. You must be leaving the UK in search of work, and register as seeking work with the Spanish authorities within seven days of your last claim for Jobseeker's Allowance in the UK. You must contact your Jobcentre Plus office or Jobcentre before leaving, and complete the appropriate forms if you have not done so already to claim benefit. If you cannot find employment during that 13-week period, then you will have to return to the UK if you wish to continue to receive benefit. You are only entitled to claim Jobseeker's Allowance abroad for one 13-week period between periods of employment.

Attendance Allowance and Disability Living Allowance are not normally payable once you move abroad permanently.

If you are living in Spain but remain liable to pay UK income tax and National Insurance, you or your spouse are entitled to claim Child Benefit from the UK authorities. This is not means tested.

Entitlement to Spanish state benefits

For those not in receipt of benefits when they move to Spain, but who subsequently become entitled, the rules are different. Generally, you are insured by the country in which you work and pay tax and social contributions. Those who work in more than one EU country are governed by the rules of the country in which they live.

If you lose your job in Spain you are entitled to claim unemployment benefit from the Spanish authorities. They take into account the National Insurance contributions you have paid in the UK or other EU country. You should ask your Jobcentre Plus office or Jobcentre for the forms you would need to enable you to make any claim in Spain. Further information is available from Instituto Nacional del Empleo (INEM), tel: 915 76 89 02, Web site: www.inem.es

Importing your belongings

There are no restrictions on EU citizens bringing personal belongings into the country, although you are required to have an inventory that can be produced to customs officials. Non-EU nationals intending to reside in Spain are required to pay VAT on any possessions that they bring into the country, and that they have owned for less than 6 months and on all belongings brought into the country 12 months after their residence began (there are some exceptions). To import personal belongings, non-EU nationals are required to make an application to the head of the customs office (*La Dirección General de Aduanas*) in the area in which they will be living, to allow the goods to enter Spain free of duty. Reputable international removal companies are familiar with the various procedures and should advise you of the necessary details. You are required to make a list, in duplicate, of all your possessions, with translations in Spanish, and pay a deposit equal to about half the estimated value of your belongings. You then have 12 months in which to obtain a residence permit and to produce this to the customs officials, together with a request for the return of your deposit. Failure to apply in time results in the loss of the deposit! Those non-EU citizens with a second home (*vivienda secundaria*) should follow the same procedure, but have two years in which to apply for the return of their deposit.

Spain has similar restrictions to the UK in relation to importing such items as drugs and firearms. There are also regulations relating to the importing of animals, animal products, plants and items with a possible military use. If in doubt, you should ask for advice from Spanish customs.

Pets

To take a pet to Spain, no permit is required from the Spanish authorities, but you will need an export certificate. The certificate is issued after examination by a veterinary surgeon in the UK, and must be issued not more than 15 days before your pet enters Spain. The form for this is obtainable from the Department for Environment, Food and Rural Affairs (DEFRA), tel: 08459 335577, which will also send you a summary of the regulations governing the importing of your animal into Spain. There is also a Web site explaining the procedures at www.defra.gov.uk. In addition you will need a certificate of vaccination against rabies. You must travel with your pet or meet it at the port of entry. Dogs and cats must be at least three months old and you may only import a maximum of three cats or dogs at one time. (See Appendix 4 for approved carriers and routes for pets to Spain.)

While there is generally no difficulty regarding taking your pet to Spain, complications arise if you wish to bring it back into the UK. Advice and assistance is available from the Pets helpline run by DEFRA (contact details as above). In brief, you will need to have your pet fitted with a microchip and then vaccinated against rabies. You will then have to arrange to have a blood test to check that the vaccine has been effective. The whole procedure takes about eight months, so you will need to plan ahead. Check with the centre that is to test your animal's blood how long they are currently taking to return results (there is a wide variation – I have been told that the Institut für Virologie, Frankfurter Strasse 107, D-35392 Giessen in Germany, tel: 00 49 641 99 38350, returns results reasonably quickly). Just before leaving, you will need to have your pet treated for ticks and tapeworm. There are relatively few companies that have made arrangements permitting them to bring pets into the UK (a list is contained in Appendix 4). More routes are anticipated in the coming years and you should contact DEFRA (see above) for information.

Your car

European Union citizens are entitled to bring their EU-registered car into Spain without completing any formalities. However, the car must not be used by its owner, or any other person, for more than six months in any calendar year. Broadly similar rules apply to boats. Those spending more than six months a year in Spain are deemed resident, and therefore must undertake the procedures involved in registering their vehicle in Spain. Traditionally the Spanish police have been very lenient with those who continue to run their foreign-registered cars in Spain for prolonged periods. In recent years, however, foreigners have been increasingly stopped by the police and asked for proof that their car is only used for six months in any year. Accordingly, if you are a non-resident and run a car in Spain you would be well advised to have your passport stamped, or to retain your travel documents so that you can prove how long you have been in Spain. If you are unable to provide this proof, you may be faced with fines in the region of 2,000 euros, and be required either to import the car formally into Spain, or to take it out of the country.

Non-EU citizens are also entitled to run their foreign registered car in Spain for up to six months in a calendar year, but are required to undergo a 'sealing' procedure when the vehicle is not in use. You should notify the customs officials, the *aduano,* when a period of non-use is to begin. The civil guard will then come to put tape across the steering wheel to prevent its use. If you require the car for leaving the country, or become entitled to drive it again, you contact the customs officials who can then unseal it, and you can then drive it in Spain for a further six months. The costs involved in having your vehicle sealed and unsealed are modest.

For EU citizens there are no duties on cars purchased in EU countries. Non-EU citizens will not have to pay VAT either, providing they paid VAT in the country of origin, and have owned it for at least six months. They must start the procedure for importing the vehicle within one month of the issue of their residence card, and be able to prove residence in Spain. The latter can be done by making a declaration of your intention to settle in Spain to the Spanish consulate in your home country, or to your own consulate on arrival in Spain. It is not unknown for people to receive their residence card some weeks after the date of its issue, and accordingly application for exemption from tax should be made at the same time as the application for a residence card.

UK registration documents should be returned to the DVLA, from whom a Certificate of Permanent Export (V561) should be obtained. You will need to obtain a road-worthiness certificate for your right hand drive vehicle from a Spanish MOT centre (known as an ITV), and have your headlights adjusted.

If you are non-resident, then you can only obtain a car in Spain with temporary tourist plates that are valid for six months in any one year, and which are required to be renewed annually.

Traffic regulations now require drivers to keep certain equipment in their cars, namely a set of bulbs and a spare tyre, together with the tools required to replace them, and two warning triangles bearing a round symbol E9 and the code 27R03. A fine of about 90 euros is payable for failure to comply with this latter regulation. The use of mobile telephones is prohibited while driving. A completely hands-free set is permitted, but headsets are not. Radar detectors are also against the law.

A UK driving licence (green) is not accepted, save for tourists, who should obtain a translation in Spanish from the Spanish Embassy in London. An EU licence (pink) is of course valid. Holders should register with the Provincial Traffic Headquarters within six months of arrival in Spain when they will be given details of when they must apply to renew their licence.

If you are using your foreign-registered car in Spain, you need to extend your home country insurance cover to Spain. The insurance company should issue you with a 'green card'. Those with Spanish-registered vehicles must take out a policy in Spain. There are a number of differences between the regulations in the UK and Spain governing motor insurance. You should ensure that you fully understand the extent of the cover under any policy you are contemplating taking out. An important point is that even under apparently fully comprehensive policies, you will only receive a proportion of the vehicle's value should it need to be written off. Take care also that you comply with the conditions contained in the policy, including the time limits and other provisions for the reporting of claims. As in the UK insurance is considerably cheaper with a higher excess.

If you have an accident, ensure that you obtain the name, address and insurance company of the other driver. Contact your insurance agent as quickly as possible. You have two months in which to bring charges against the other driver.

As part of its campaign to take old cars off its roads, the Spanish government grants a subsidy of up to about 750 euros off the car registration tax for those purchasing a new vehicle and scrapping their old car. The highest grants apply where the car to be scrapped runs on regular leaded petrol.

An annual vehicle tax is payable to your local council, based on the horse-power of the vehicle, with the tax payable starting from about 60 euros. The receipt for this tax should be kept in your car, together with the registration papers and insurance receipt to provide to the police if you are stopped.

All cars over four years old have to undergo a test, the ITV or *Inspección Técnica de Vehículos*, which is similar to the annual MOT in the UK.

The railway system

The railway system is known as RENFE (*Red Nacional de Ferrocarriles Españoles*). The TALGO is a fast, comfortable inter-city train, but has been outclassed by the newer AVE (*alta velocidad española*), a high-speed train reminiscent of the French TGV, linking Madrid with Seville, Madrid with Barcelona and Barcelona with the south of France. Train fares are reduced on *dias azules* (blue days).

Taking and transferring money to Spain

There are no restrictions on transferring money to Spain, though it is advisable to keep records in case you need to prove that the money does not arise from income earned in Spain. Those travelling to Spain carrying more than 6,000 euros in cash (*efectivo*) are required to make a declaration on entry into Spain, stating the purpose for which the money is being brought into the country. Residents wishing to travel abroad with more than 6,000 euros in cash are also supposed to make a customs declaration. You can obtain the form from the bank from which you obtained the cash. If you wish to carry more than 30,000 euros you are required to fill in a different form and to seek authority from the *Dirección General de Transacciones Exteriores.* Permission is generally granted.

Once you have a Spanish bank account, it is easy to make transfers from your UK account into your Spanish account. UK banks normally tell you that it will take up to five working days. In practice the transfer in euros may be credited to your Spanish account more quickly than this, but in some cases it can take longer. Under new European regulations the receiving bank is not allowed to make a charge for receiving sums in euros. Your UK bank may make a charge of £20–30 per transfer, irrespective of the amount. Changing to a Spanish bank that is part of the same group as your UK bank may significantly reduce the charge.

There are no restrictions on transferring money out of Spain, but you will have to declare all transfers over 600 euros on a 'B' form, stating the identity of the recipient and the purpose of the payment. The Spanish government requires this information in its efforts to restrict money laundering, and to prevent tax evasion. A resident who receives transfers from abroad is similarly required to inform his or her bank of the identity and address of the sender and the reason for the payment.

A Spanish bank account

You will need a Spanish bank account, probably a current account (*cuenta corriente*). Non-residents can open a non-resident account (*cuenta extranjera*). You will be provided with a chequebook (*talonario*), although cheques are not used with the same frequency as in the UK. Note that post-dating a cheque is ineffective, it can be drawn on immediately. Many Spaniards ask for cheques to be made out to the *portador*, ie cash, to avoid declaring it for tax purposes.

Residents have 15 per cent of interest earned deducted direct for tax purposes, though you can recover this if you are not liable for tax on these sums. Bank charges in Spain are higher than in most other European countries, even for routine operations. Commission on transfers out of Spain vary tremendously. If you are likely to make regular transfers abroad, a bank's charges for this service should be one of the factors you consider when deciding upon your choice of bank.

As with UK banks, notify your Spanish bank immediately of any loss or suspected theft of your chequebook or card – you are responsible for any loss until you do.

Complaints about banking services should first be addressed to the local manager. If he or she does not resolve your complaint to your satisfaction then you can take the matter to your bank's *Defensor del Cliente*. This frequently results in a decision in the client's favour. If you are still dissatisfied you can take the matter to the Bank of Spain's *Servicio de Reclamaciones*.

Household insurance

As in the UK, you should insure your property for its full worth, taking into account the value of the land, but also the cost of demolition and rebuilding. Similarly, with contents, you should insure their full value if you are to be certain of having a claim met in full. Your insurers need to know if the property is vacant for much of the year and if you are letting the property. If this is the case, the premiums will be higher, but failure to notify your insurer of the situation will result in the disallowance of relevant claims.

Claims normally have to be submitted within a very short time of an incident so you should check the terms of the policy. Thefts and break-ins also have to be reported to the police as a condition of the policy, usually within 24 hours.

Communications: the telephone and postal system, fax, and the Internet

The Spanish postal service is extremely variable, and deliveries of mail in Spain are often slow. Those who live near Gibraltar will find that mail posted there to the UK arrives more quickly than if it is posted in Spain.

Queues in Spanish post offices are notorious. Post offices in Madrid and the main cities are generally open from 9.00 am to 10.00 pm or even later from Monday to Friday, and on Saturday mornings. Elsewhere opening hours are more restricted, with many post offices still closing at 2.30 pm and mail received after 1.00 pm having to wait until the next day. It is often possible to collect parcels after the post office has closed.

Stamps can also be purchased at shops licensed to sell tobacco. It is worth considering having a PO Box or *apartado de correos*. This can mean that you receive letters several days earlier than if they are sent to a conventional address. The cost of having a PO box is modest, and in any event you will need to visit the post office to collect any large parcels, as in most areas these are not delivered by the postman. Try to post letters at a main post office, and in particular avoid using post boxes.

The Spanish telephone operator Telefónica lost its state monopoly about 10 years ago, and telecommunications in Spain have since changed dramatically, with more choice, lower prices and shorter delays. A mobile phone can be operational within 24 hours of its purchase. Public telephones are still difficult to find in remoter areas. If you need to use one, ask at a hotel or restaurant. Most newsagents have a fax facility. The number for the local police is 1092 and for the operator is 1004. If you wish to take your UK mobile phone to Spain, contact your service provider. It can be quite expensive.

Spain has lagged behind the UK in the spread and popularity of the Internet. That said, it has grown rapidly in recent years and most large businesses, government departments and local councils have Web sites providing a vast quantity of information. Some basic Internet vocabulary is included in Appendix 3.

Television and satellite

There are several Spanish television channels, but many foreign residents prefer to receive English language programmes. There are several ways in which to obtain UK TV and radio programmes via satellite. A number of channels can be received free of charge using a receiver that you can purchase from a dealer or electrical retailer. Some Britons in Spain receive BBC 1, BBC 2, ITV, Channel 4, Channel 5 and Sky by using a receiver available from specialists and a card from the UK. This is, in fact, unlawful as licensing and copyright laws restrict the use of the card to the UK. Details of suppliers and installers are prominent in the local English language newspapers.

Welcome to Spain

If you wish to integrate fully into Spanish life, and especially if you live in the more rural areas, you must make contacts among the local Spanish community. Even if you are the only English-speaking family, you are probably not the only newcomers in the area – there are many Germans and Scandinavians, as well as those Spaniards who leave Madrid in favour of a home in the countryside, for example.

There are steps you can take to ease the transition to your new home and environment. Prior to purchasing, or indeed renting, you would do well to introduce yourselves to your immediate neighbours in order to ask them about the property and the neighbourhood. Once you have moved in, renew the acquaintance. You have the perfect pretext in that you are new to the area and can ask them for information or advice about the area or alterations and improvements that they have made to their property.

There will be local sports and cultural associations in which you can participate. If you have children at the local school, you will find that they soon make friends. This will bring you into contact with other parents in the area, some of them keen for their children to establish links with English-speaking people in the hope that this will help them in acquiring what remains by far the most important world language.

Most villages have regular festivals. Each local school will have its annual events. Integration inevitably requires participation. If you are in a village, do carry out some of your shopping locally. Do buy and look at the local newspaper. It is not only about becoming part of the community, but it may be the first notification you have that a new motorway is planned that will directly affect your daily life and/or the value of your property. On this note, some expatriates have taken an active part in campaigning on local issues. Foreign residents have the right to vote in municipal elections and, in some, the British and other foreign residents form a potentially significant group of the electorate.

There are many English-speaking associations throughout Spain, especially in the more popular areas. They are mainly British, but include US, Irish, South African, Canadian and Australian clubs and associations and some that are specifically Scottish or Welsh. They range from churches and religious groups, to cricket clubs, women's groups, activities for children and retired servicemen's associations. There are also various UK and joint cultural centres and groups – most notably the British Council. Friendships are often quick to form among the expatriate community. Whatever your age and circumstances, you may find others' help and advice indispensable, including in relation to finding employment.

You may be reluctant to immerse yourself completely among expatriates. One possibility is to participate in the joint groups.

Speaking and learning the language

In many parts of Spain it is very easy to live in an almost totally English-speaking environment in which you rarely have to speak a word of Spanish. However, if you are truly to settle, you really do need to have some understanding of the language. Indeed, it is essential if you wish to obtain employment with a Spanish employer. It is important, too, if you are confidently to handle emergency situations and for your dealings with the various administrative bodies.

In fact Spain has four languages: Castilian (the language generally known as 'Spanish'), Basque, Catalan and Gallego (the language of Galicia). These are all distinct separate languages, although all derived from Latin, save for Basque, the origins of which are the subject of some academic dispute.

Castilian is the first language of the majority of Spain, including Madrid, and is also (broadly) the language spoken in the 20 or so Spanish speaking countries throughout the world. Though derived from Latin, the language has obvious Arabic influences, as is apparent from many place names that have Arabic roots. Castilian has a variety of regional accents, and that of the northern Spanish is said to be the easiest for foreigners to follow. It is also the language of Andalusia, and hence of the Costa del Sol and the Costa de la Luz, and also of the Canary Islands.

Catalan is spoken by about 9 million people, mostly in Catalonia, Valencia and the Balearic Islands, and is spoken across the social spectrum. It is the language of Barcelona and the Costa Brava, Costa Dorado and Costa del Azahar and to a lesser extent the Costa Blanca. Basque is limited to the eastern end of the North Atlantic coast. It is notoriously difficult to learn. Legend has it that after seven years of trying to learn to speak Basque the Devil was only able to say 'yes' and 'no'. When he realized that he had confused the two words he gave up! Gallego is understood by most of the 2.75 million inhabitants of the north western corner of Spain. However, today it is primarily the language of the rural areas, and Castilian Spanish is dominant elsewhere.

There is no doubt that Spanish is a much easier language than French, the traditional choice of foreign language for most of us in our school days. There is, of course, no better place to learn it than in Spain itself. There are many different courses. A detailed list can be found at The Spanish Directory: Learn in Spain at www.europa-pages.com. Many courses will be in target language only (Spanish), with no English spoken. The most well-known organization is the *Instituto Cervantes*, which is akin to the British Council, or L'Institut Français for France, and runs courses in all the main cities. There are (expensive) total immersion options available in which you spend a period of time in a Spanish family, attending courses during the day.

For the serious student, there are many qualifications that can be gained. Study for O level and A level Spanish is possible via correspondence courses with the National Extension College, as is the External Degree in Spanish Studies at London University. The Open University has courses for complete beginners up to a Diploma in Spanish, in which the level of language is equivalent to that learnt at a traditional university. There are various examination centres in Spain, although you should check with the individual examining body.

The best way to advance your Spanish is obviously to use it. Making Spanish friends will prove invaluable to this end. So, too, is the Spanish media. Watching and listening to television is a must, but ensure that your viewing is *selective*. Avoid the most difficult programmes to follow, such as chat shows (everybody always talks at the same time!) and Spanish TV series. Translations of English-language films or television series are invariably in standard Spanish and you seldom have to cope with the difficulties of regional accents. You will also be more familiar with what is being shown pictorially (such as courtroom scenes, police investigations, lifestyles and so on). The programmes will, accordingly be easier to follow (and enjoy) as well as to learn from. Obviously, you can learn more by adopting a systematic approach. For example, the same words appear frequently and it is helpful to make a note of them. If you record the programme, you can replay it to hear something that you have missed. News bulletins are also worth watching – newsreaders tend to speak clearly and are accordingly easier to understand. News is repeated throughout the day, so if you did not pick something up the first time around, you will have another opportunity to do so, perhaps listening to a different newsreader.

Radio is inevitably more difficult to follow. However, time in your car could be usefully spent learning the language and, if you are not listening to Spanish language tapes, consider a news channel, especially on long journeys. Consider listening to the BBC News or, preferably, a local English radio station that has local and national news. This will give you an idea of the main news items and help you to follow them on Spanish radio. You will find that many people try to speak to you in English. You should politely persist in speaking Spanish. They may well be simply trying to impress a third party and it may be that their knowledge of English is limited to only a few words. If so, it will not compare to your own level of Spanish after you have been in the country for a while.

If you wish to study the language prior to moving to Spain, consider the courses run by the *Instituto Cervantes,* which has centres in London, Manchester and Dublin. These are cultural centres where you can also learn more about Spain and Spanish culture, see Spanish films and meet Spanish people living in the UK or Ireland.

The time of day

To most other Europeans, the Spanish day is two hours or more behind that in the rest of Europe. Lunch takes place at about 2.00 pm (or even an hour later in Andalusia) and dinner from 10.00 pm. Spaniards go to bed later than the rest of Europe. Literally the expression *mediodia* means midday, but is invariably used to refer to about lunchtime – ie from 2.00 pm, during which a siesta is often taken. Most shops open at 9.00 am or 10.00 am and close at 1.30 pm for lunch, generally re-opening from 4.00 pm. The larger stores do not close over lunch.

Formalities

In many ways the Spanish remain more formal than the British or other Anglo-Saxons. This is most apparent in business and other correspondence. Remember that women do not change their name when they marry, so a husband and wife bear different surnames. *Don* or *Dona* often precedes a person's name. Someone who we would refer to as Mr Richard Smith, whose mother's maiden name was Jones, would be referred to as Senor Don Richard Smith Jones. When addressing letters, the road name is written first, followed by the number – 45 Barcelona Street would be written Calle Barcelona 45.

Your neighbours and you

The key to minimizing problems is always to attempt to establish a good relationship with your neighbours from the outset, whatever their nationality, even if you are going to keep them at arm's length. At some point, you may well need each other – especially if you live some distance from shops and other facilities. If a dispute does arise, do your utmost to settle disagreements without recourse to the courts, perhaps asking a third party to act as a type of arbiter (such as an *abogado*). Litigation may only fuel animosities and leave both sides with substantial legal bills.

You have no right to complain about a nuisance that is no more than a norm for the neighbourhood (such as church bells that have been rung for centuries, but which might lead to mental instability if you were unwise enough to purchase the house next door). This is merely a characteristic of the neighbourhood that you are obliged to accept. For abnormal nuisances, however, there are rules and regulations governing such matters as noise and pollution.

Taking Spanish nationality

Before applying to become a Spanish citizen (or indeed a citizen of any country) you should ensure that you are aware of both the advantages and the disadvantages. Your country of origin will not be prepared to interfere with any demands made upon you by your adopted country, such as military service, or indeed conscription.

According to the Home Office, Her Majesty has no objection to British subjects applying for citizenship of a foreign state or states, without losing their British nationality. Most English-speaking countries including Ireland, the United States, Canada, Australia and New Zealand take the same permissive stance. Spain, however, forbids dual nationality by requiring applicants to renounce their existing citizenship. If you are British, you will have to make a formal application to the British government to renounce your British citizenship.

Spain also insists on a period of 10 years' residency in Spain before a foreigner is entitled to become a citizen (in France, for example, the period is only 5 years). This does not apply to those born in Spain, or who marry a Spaniard, and a shorter period is also applicable for citizens of South American countries.

There is clearly a significant advantage for a non-European citizen in obtaining a Spanish passport, namely the entitlement to live and work anywhere within the European Union. However, citizens of the various

English-speaking countries may well be entitled to live in any country of the European Union, by virtue of their Irish roots. US citizens, Canadians, South Africans, Australians, New Zealanders and those of any other nationality who can establish that they have one grandparent who was both an Irish national, and born in either the Republic of Ireland or Northern Ireland, have the right to an Irish passport. No period of residence in Ireland is required. Irish citizenship of course brings with it entitlement to live and work anywhere within the European Union, without having to renounce your existing citizenship, as you would do if you became a Spanish citizen.

If you do decide to take on Spanish nationality, do remember that it comes with no guarantee of having a sense of belonging. When all is said and done, having a sense of being *at home* is perhaps the most important element of all.

Further information as to the obtaining of Spanish citizenship can be obtained from a Spanish consulate. Information on how this will affect your present national status can be obtained from your embassy in Madrid, or its local consulate. A list of addresses and telephone numbers of the various consulates is included in Appendix 1. If you decide to apply for Spanish citizenship you will need your birth certificate, your parents' birth certificates and their marriage certificate, together with translations of all these documents authenticated by the Spanish consulate, and also proof that you have resided in Spain for 10 years. The procedure takes about 12 months.

10 Letting and selling your Spanish home

If you do not intend to occupy your Spanish home full-time, you may wish to cover part of your costs by renting it out. There are several options.

Holiday lettings

If you only intend to spend short periods in your property, you could consider trying to let it out to other holiday visitors during the holiday seasons. Spain remains a top destination for tourists and, in many areas, the holiday letting season can last for several months of the year. In the most popular resorts, most notably on the Costa de Sol, there is a substantial unmet demand for both holiday and longer-term lettings. The location of the property is obviously important for its letting potential. It should also have the basic facilities.

Even if you intend to live in the property more or less continuously, you may still wish to consider letting for short periods. On the Costa del Sol, for example, it should be possible to let a home for the whole of the summer or during August and go to live elsewhere or take an extended holiday. The rental income during this busy season is several times the monthly mortgage instalments.

Many Spanish property owners manage lettings themselves, placing advertisements on a number of Internet sites or newspapers and magazines in the UK or, indeed, in Spain. If you work in a large organization, such as a local authority, hospital or private company, or have a good friend who does, you may be able to circulate details among the employees. Your own small Internet site (at a modest cost of about £400) is also worth considering. If you are not going to be on site when your property is being let, remember that you will need someone who can arrange to have the property cleaned for you, deal with hand-overs and any emergencies that may arise. Ideally, you should also have that person place some basic supplies, such as fresh bread, butter, milk and mineral water, in the property in preparation for the arrival of your guests.

Alternatively, you can instruct one of a number of Spanish or English-speaking management agents. Management agents charge a hefty commission and vary tremendously in the quality of the service they provide. You will need to keep a close eye on them to ensure that they are keeping the property as fully let as possible, and are providing a good service to your clients (especially with regard to keeping the property clean). Insist on being provided with a week-by-week schedule of rental income with contact details of tenants – some agencies have been known to keep part of the rental income for themselves during peak periods or to fail to inform proprietors of a letting during the low season. If you know someone who lives nearby who can make spot checks, so much the better.

There is also nothing to stop you entering into an agreement in English, and this is frequently done for self-catering holiday flats. A landlord wishing to let on a longer-term basis, however, cannot escape the protection granted by Spanish law (see below) by granting a tenancy in English, even if the agreement is signed by a UK tenant in the UK prior to leaving for Spain.

Short-term lettings are regulated by the provincial governments. Accordingly, the rules governing letting, and the extent to which they are enforced, vary from area to area. The provincial authorities may inspect properties to decide whether they are suitable for letting, and may impose conditions, for example in relation to the alteration of a fire exit. You should consult a lawyer as to the terms of any letting, the consequences in relation to your income tax liability and your overall tax position.

The return that you can expect from renting out your Spanish property will depend on a number of factors, not least the effort that you put into finding clients, the location of the property, accessibility from the UK, and attractiveness of the property. You should prepare a brief information pack. Of crucial importance are good directions to the property – if these are complicated, then potential clients may be put off. In your description of the area, you should include references to the main tourist attractions, particularly those in close proximity to the property, as well as local restaurants, supermarkets, banks, markets, pharmacies, doctors and hospitals. A good map showing the property, main landmarks and attractions is essential. The best bookings are from clients who wish to return.

Longer-term lettings

Before letting out your property on a longer-term letting, I recommend that you read Chapter 3, which sets out the main considerations in detail, albeit from a tenant's perspective.

The first point for a prospective landlord to remember is that the long-term rental of properties is subject to extensive regulation under Spanish law. These provisions override the terms of any written or oral rental contract. Tenants have rather more rights than in the UK, at least when it comes to security of tenure. Under the present Law of Urban Lettings (*Ley de Arrendamientos Urbanos*), the law provides that in contracts *de vivienda,* ie rental contracts for one year or more, the tenant has an automatic right to renew the tenancy for up to five years. Accordingly, if you enter into a two-year agreement with a tenant, he or she will have a right to remain in the property for up to a further three years. During this five-year period you are entitled to increase the rent each year, but only in line with inflation. Once the five-year period has expired, the landlord then has the freedom to increase the rent as he or she wishes.

During this five-year period, it is impossible to obtain possession of the property if the tenant wishes to remain, save on fairly narrow grounds, such as substantial rent arrears or damage to the property. Even in these cases, obtaining possession can be a lengthy process and the courts may refuse to grant you possession, giving the tenant one or more opportunities to remedy his or her default.

If a landlord wishes to obtain possession of his or her property after the five-year period has expired, he or she must notify the tenant (in writing, from a notary) well before the expiry of the five-year period. Failure to do so can mean that the tenancy is extended for a further two years on the same terms. Even if the landlord has given the requisite notice, he or she cannot simply proceed to evict the tenant – he or she must first obtain a court order for possession.

When you let out a property on a longer-term letting, you are entitled to demand a deposit of one month's rent on the signing of the rental agreement. The deposit is paid as a guarantee of the condition of the property and the other risks taken by the proprietor in letting the property. At the end of the rental, the deposit is returned to the tenant, less your costs of rectifying any damage to the property and any unpaid rent.

The deposit can be paid to an agency, rather than the landlord. The agency should not release the deposit to either party without the consent of you both.

Before a tenant moves in, you should arrange to draw up a document setting out the condition of the property (see Chapter 3, and the checklist included in that chapter), and have the tenant sign an inventory of the items included in the rental.

As a landlord, you are responsible for maintaining the structure of the building, including the roof and boundaries, stairs, shutters and windows, boiler and chimney. The tenant is responsible for running repairs, such as minor works of maintenance to prevent the building falling into disrepair – tasks such as painting, replacing windowpanes, cleaning and minor repairs to pipework, taps and radiators, replacing the odd broken floor tile.

The nightmare tenant

Whether you are letting your property for short-term holiday lets or for longer periods, there is always the risk of encountering a tenant who will not leave or only does so after causing extensive damage to your property. You can take out insurance against such eventualities. There are various policies available with different levels of cover.

Property insurance

You should make your insurers aware that you are letting the property and the type of lettings involved. Failure to do so may result in a claim being disallowed.

Income tax

Income from Spanish property, even rental paid into your UK bank account, is subject to income tax. In 2003 the government reduced the proportion of rental income subject to income tax to 50 per cent, in an effort to encourage the rental market. In addition you are entitled to deduct numerous expenses against your rental income. In practice many residents pay little tax on their rental income.

If you are a non-resident you are liable to pay income tax of 25 per cent on *all* your property rental income – the reduction introduced in 2003 applies only to residents.

Right of first refusal

Remember that if you wish to sell your rented property you are obliged to give a tenant the right of first refusal (the *tanteo y retracto*). You should notify the tenant, in writing, of the sale price, and the conditions of sale. If you fail to do this, a tenant has the right to have the sale annulled, and to purchase the property at the price recorded on the contract for sale.

Selling your property

Selling property in Spain generally takes longer than in the UK. You can seek assistance and obtain a valuation from an estate agent, or, as many foreign property owners and Spaniards do, seek to sell the property yourself. It is fair to say that of those who try the latter option, a good number of them wish they had instructed an agent. Estate agents' commission is generally between 5 and 10 per cent, plus VAT. It is usually included in the advertised purchase price, and is something that you can negotiate. It is common practice for vendors to instruct several agents. The agent's fees are fully deductible against the increase in the value of the property, for the calculation of your capital gains tax liability.

Many vendors, even those who instructed their own lawyer when they purchased, decide not to obtain legal representation on their sale. It is true that there are generally fewer complications on a sale than on a purchase. In my opinion, however, vendors should seriously consider instructing a lawyer. He or she is well positioned to advise on your capital gains tax liability, and on any problems that may arise, such as how to deal with unwelcome points not picked up when you purchased the property, and the failure of the purchaser to complete on time, or at all (see Chapter 4). Often purchasers may put forward proposals to pay by instalments or to rent the property with an option to buy. Clearly if you have other prospective purchasers in the wings, or are not in a hurry to sell, you will probably reject such proposals. In reality you may wish to give them serious consideration, though never let anyone into possession until you have the full purchase price, or have discussed this with your lawyer and are happy with his or her advice. You would be well advised to insist that any option to purchase represents a significant proportion of the value of the property (it can be deducted against the price if the other party proceeds with a purchase), and even better advised to instruct your own lawyer. This may also be an opportune time to consider up-dating your Spanish and/or UK wills. Your lawyer's fees on a sale should not be more than 1 per cent of the sale price, and your best course of action may well be to negotiate a reduction in your estate agent's fees to cover this.

Remember that, although historically it was the vendor who paid the *plus valia* (not to be confused with capital gains tax) and the notary's fees, it is increasingly common for the sale contract, drafted by your estate agent if you have instructed one, to require the purchaser to pay these.

Practicalities

Your estate agent and lawyer, as well as prospective purchasers, will want to see:

- Your copy of the *escritura publica* showing your title to the property.
- A receipt for payments of the *impuesto sobre bienes inmuebles* (IBI) or property tax. In addition to confirming payment of the tax, the receipt carries the reference number of the *Catastro* that the notaire will need on completion.
- A copy of the *Certificado Catastral*. This contains a detailed description of the property and will help a prospective purchaser

understand the location of the boundaries, and what is and is not included in the sale.

▌ Your income tax declaration. If you are a resident, the notary will need to see this, so that he or she can be sure that the purchaser is not obliged to retain 5 per cent of the sale price, as would be the case for a non-resident.

▌ If you are selling a property within a development, the rules of the Community of Property Owners, and receipts for the annual charges.

▌ Copies of your utility bills. The purchaser may wish to see how much it costs to run the property, and have confirmation that the bills are paid up to date.

On completion, insist on a banker's draft in your own name. If you will be unable to attend at the notary's office, you can appoint someone you trust as your attorney. It is easier and cheaper to appoint an attorney while you are in Spain, as if you do it in your home country, you will either have to find a Spanish-speaking notary, or have the document prepared at the Spanish consulate.

Capital gains tax

When selling a property both residents and non-residents are liable to tax on the capital gain. Non-residents pay 35 per cent, and purchasers from a non-resident are obliged to retain 5 per cent of the purchase price and pay this to the *Hacienda*, on account of the vendor's tax liability. You have six months to claim this back, although you may have to wait up to another year before you receive it. If you are resident in Spain your capital gain is taxed at up to 15 per cent and is taken into account when your income tax is calculated.

A number of people are exempt from capital gains tax. These include those selling a property purchased before 1987, residents who are 65 and above who have lived in a property for three years or more, and residents who are using the entire proceeds to finance another main home in Spain.

The tax is calculated on a sliding scale – the longer you have owned the property, the lower the tax. Some of the expenses that you may have incurred in relation to the property will be deductible from your gain. It is obviously important to keep a file of receipts and bills as they can reduce your apparent gain considerably and may well even extinguish any liability.

In the past vendors have persuaded purchasers to declare a purchase at an undervalue so that they can reduce their liability to capital gains. This is far less common with the increasing vigilance of the tax authorities following the 1989 Law of Public Fees. Under-valuations of 20 per cent or more attract penalties. The *Hacienda* will be happy to provide you with an estimate of their opinion of the value of your property if you contact the regional *oficina liquidora*, although if you declare the correct sale price you should not fall foul of the regulations.

Education and health

The face of Spanish education has undergone a dramatic transformation in the last 10 years or so, with a substantial improvement in the standard offered by both private and state schools. Education is compulsory from the age of 6 to 16.

Pre-school education (*educación infantil*)

Education does not become compulsory in Spain until children are six years old. Many parents of British and foreign children choose to send their children to Spanish nursery schools (*guarderias*), even though they may have already decided to opt for some form of English-speaking, bilingual or international school for the primary and secondary years. Firstly, these nursery schools are not very expensive. Secondly, attendance enables children to learn to speak Spanish during the years that they are most receptive to acquiring a second language. A significant number of foreign parents keep their children at Spanish primary schools, and make the move to an English education when their children are aged 11.

Education for the under six is divided into two cycles, up to three years old, and from age three to six. The institutions offering pre-school education are subject to control by the state, which sets down regulations governing what is taught, and how the institutions are run. Some are state operated.

Choices for primary and secondary education

Your choices will depend very much on where you live. International, bilingual and British educational options are greater in and around

Madrid, Barcelona, and the Costa del Sol. The larger towns and cities have a good range of private Spanish schools. The possibilities are as follows.

State schools

Education in state school (*escuela publica, colegio publico*) is free, though parents are responsible for the cost of books, and school materials such as exercise books, pens, pencils, crayons and so on, as well as for the cost of extra-curricular activities. About two-thirds of Spanish children attend state schools, with the rest attending some form of private school.

As with all types of school, standards in state schools vary considerably. In some areas, the presence of significant numbers of British or other foreign families is putting a considerable strain on school resources, and on the relationship between the foreigners and the local Spanish parents. Frequently the British children speak no Spanish on arrival in Spain, and Spanish parents are legitimately concerned about the disproportionate time spent by teaching staff in helping foreign children, and the detrimental effects on the progress of Spanish children. Among the children themselves, in some schools animosities develop between the Spanish children and foreign children, creating discipline problems. You may find that your child's progress, both in Spanish and across the board, is better in a state school where there are relatively few other English-speaking children.

If your child is to attend state school, it must be within a certain distance of your home. Accordingly, it would be wise to make enquiries about the local school, and indeed see if the head-teacher is willing to meet you, *before* you commit yourself to a property purchase.

In theory the procedure for admitting your child into a Spanish state school is somewhat complicated, long-winded and should be put into motion before you leave the UK. Your child is supposed to be interviewed, and could be asked to complete an examination to assess his or her level of Spanish. A child's education records are 'supposed' to be translated into Spanish, a requirement that can be quite costly, and then 'convalidated' or assessed. I have seen it stated that a child will not be accepted until the convalidation papers have been issued.

In practice, however, the position is far more relaxed, and many parents state that they simply contacted the local school and spoke to the head-teacher. You will, however, need to provide your child's birth certificate or passport, proof of your child's immunization, and proof of residence such as a utility bill, rental agreement or *escritura*. Note, however, that in popular areas there is a risk that your child may not be admitted to your local school if the school is full. Enrolment usually starts from March/April for the September term.

Further information concerning state schools can be found on the Web site of the Spanish Ministry of Education www.mec.es/educacion. In any event it would be wise to contact the Ministry's London office on 020 772 72462 several months before you leave the UK.

Private Spanish schools

A large number of private schools (*escuelas privados, colegios privados*) in Spain are Catholic schools. Many private schools are assisted by the state (*colegios concertados*). The standard of education is generally higher than for state schools, and your child is more sheltered. Fees are lower than for the international schools, and in the areas most popular with foreign residents a significant proportion of children at these schools is foreign. A major advantage of sending your child to a private school is that he or she does not have to change schools if you move house, for example if you rent initially and only buy after living in the area for 12 months or so. There are relatively few boarding schools.

International private schools

These are primarily day schools. They can be expensive, especially if you have more than one child. Fees for secondary education start from about 6,000 euros per annum, with the cost of primary education being somewhat lower. Discounts for second and third children are sometimes available. Some of these schools are essentially British, others are more US-orientated and others more internationally focused. The British-orientated schools tend to follow the UK curriculum (working to National Curriculum tests, GCSE O levels and A levels). The others prepare their students for the International Baccalaureate (in English). As with private schools in the UK and United States, extra-curricula activities are generally given far greater emphasis than in Spanish schools.

International schools generally start from nursery age and go all the way through to age 18. A list of international private schools can be found on several Web sites including www.ecis.org, www.nabss.org and www.ydelta.free.sp. General guidance can also be obtained from the ELSA-Spain (English Language Schools Association). See also Chapter 2 for regional information.

The Spanish system – state and private

The school year runs from early September until the end of June, with slight regional variations. The school day starts at 9.00 am and finishes at 4.00 pm, with a lunch-break of an hour during which a reasonably priced meal is provided, or a child can eat a packed lunch. More and more schools are deciding not to have a lunch-break in favour of an early finish at 1.30 pm or 2.00 pm.

Primary education from age 6 to 12 is divided into three cycles of two years each, with a foreign language introduced from age 8, generally English. Class size is usually limited to 25. Secondary education is divided into two cycles of two years each, ages 12 to 14 and 14 to 16. Maximum class size is intended to be 30. In both primary and secondary schools pupils who do not reach a given standard at the end of a cycle can be required to repeat a year.

Pupils who successfully complete the second cycle at secondary school are awarded the qualification of Graduate in Secondary Education. This entitles them to proceed to study for the Baccalaureate (*Bachillerato*) or be admitted to vocational training courses.

Bilingual children

I have seen claims that children under the age of eight can acquire a competence in the language within three months and near fluency after six months, while at age 11 fluency can take *up to* a year. This is contrary to the views of many experts in this field. The Doman Institute in the United

States, for example, claims that a child's capacity to acquire a second language is at its highest between the ages of three and five and drops dramatically from the age of six. In my experience, the reality is somewhere in the middle, with complete fluency in two languages requiring considerable effort on the part of the child and its parents. If you do want your children to speak fluent Spanish, it would be advisable to seek out Spanish company as much as possible and, ideally, place them in a Spanish school rather than an international school.

Fluency is not automatic and considerable effort is required on the part of parents, as well as children, to achieve it. Transferring from one language to another is a skill in itself that needs to be nurtured. Effort is also required to maintain your child's fluency in English – a language that many foreigners spend a great deal of time and money trying to acquire and which your child should not lose.

Equivalent stages of education for Spain, the UK and the United States

AGE	SPAIN	UK	US
2–5	INFANT	NURSERY	NURSERY
5–6	INFANT	Yr 1 (infants) PRIMARY	KINDERGARTEN ELEMENTARY
6–7	PRIMARY 1st CYCLE (1st)	Yr 2 (infants)	1st grade
7–8	PRIMARY 1st CYCLE (2nd)	Yr 3 (junior)	2nd grade
8–9	PRIMARY 2nd CYCLE (3rd)	Yr 4 (junior)	3rd grade
9–10	PRIMARY 2nd CYCLE (4th)	Yr 5 (junior)	4th grade
10–11	PRIMARY 3rd CYCLE (5th)	Yr 6 (junior)	5th grade
11–12	PRIMARY 3rd CYCLE (6th)	1st form	6th grade JUNIOR HIGH
12–13	SECONDARY 1st CYCLE (1st)	2nd form	7th grade
13–14	SECONDARY 1st CYCLE (2nd)	3rd form	8th grade HIGH SCHOOL
14–15	SECONDARY 2nd CYCLE (3rd)	4th form	9th grade
15–16	SECONDARY 2nd CYCLE (4th)	5th form	10th grade
16–17	BACHILLERATO (1st)	Lower 6th	11th grade
17–18	BACHILLERATO (2nd)	Upper 6th	12th grade

University education

There is a good selection of universities in Spain, including several Catholic and private universities. Entrance is by examination, the *Selectivadad*. A university education in Spain, however, takes longer than elsewhere in Europe, and for that reason many wealthy Spanish families send their children to universities abroad. Degrees in law, the sciences and humanities take four to five years, degrees in medicine, veterinary surgery, and engineering take five to six years. The academic year runs from September to June, with examinations in February and/or the end of June/July.

The Open University

The Open University's distance learning programme is available in Spain. The cost is substantially higher than in the UK. However, if you or your spouse pay UK income tax, you should be able to avoid paying the supplement. Information about the Open University's courses, and the Open University Business School can be found on their respective Web sites: www.open.ac.uk and www.oubs.open.ac.uk

Healthcare and the Spanish health system

Spaniards generally boast good health, primarily thanks to the climate, and their diet. The average life expectancy for women is 80 years, and that for men is 74, both among the highest in the world. Heart disease is nowhere near the health problem that it is in the UK. Smoking and drinking are two principal causes of illness.

The standard of healthcare in Spain has risen considerably over the last twenty years, and for the most part is of a reasonably high standard. There is a national health system, the *Instituto Nacional de Salud* or *Insalud*. Treatment and medication is free, or heavily subsidized to those who contribute to the Spanish social security scheme, though cover for dental treatment is very limited. About 75 per cent of the cost of most non-dental treatment is covered, with the balance being paid by the patient, or through private health insurance.

On the whole doctors are well trained, and hospitals have up-to-date medical equipment. The main shortcoming is in nursing care, and help to patients in the community, particularly the aged. Even in the private sector, there are, for example, very few retirement and convalescent homes, or homes for the terminally ill. Large numbers of Britons, and other foreign residents, who are no longer able to manage alone, find themselves having to return home. Spain also lags considerably behind other western European countries in its provision of facilities, including access, for the disabled. You should note that severe strain is placed on both public and indeed private health provision during August, when the holidays of medical staff coincide with peak demand in the tourist areas.

Your choice of doctor is determined by where you live, and whether you are relying on the state system. In the most popular areas, such as the Costa del Sol, there is a wide choice of doctors, available for those who are privately insured, or able to pay. Many of these doctors speak English, or are of British or other northern European nationality. On the other hand, if you are using the state system, you will initially be assigned to a general practitioner (*médico de cabecera*). You are entitled to change doctors, but your choices are restricted to another doctor in the same area whose list is not full. Almost certainly you will be consulting a Spanish doctor. You will not need to make any payment to a doctor under the state health scheme, but must present your social security card.

You do not need the referral of a general practitioner in order to consult a specialist, though you will if you wish the consultation to be paid for by the state. Similarly, many insurance policies will require a referral as a condition of paying for the fees of the specialist. The same general rule, ie obtain a referral if you are not paying yourself, applies to using the services of a nurse, physiotherapist and chiropodist.

In many towns there is a state-operated health centre, the *ambulatorio*, sometimes called the *consultorio*. You can attend the centre to register with one of the doctors there. You will be asked to show your social security card. These centres are generally quite well equipped. It is usually possible to have an X-ray taken here, or a blood sample taken for testing. Unfortunately these centres are frequently very busy, and the system of queuing at times rather chaotic and disorganized.

Your rights to medical care in Spain

If you are going to Spain for a short stay only or as a student, obtain and complete a copy of Form E111 from your local post office (it is attached to a guidance booklet). This will cover you for emergency treatment while in Spain for up to 90 days (pensioners are entitled to both emergency and routine treatment). You will be required to pay, but are entitled to recover most of the cost when you return to the UK. You will be left with having paid a modest contribution, as you would if you were living and working in Spain.

If you require a regular prescription and will need to obtain further supplies while in Spain, be sure to obtain a Form E112 and the generic name of the medication from your doctor. This will enable the Spanish chemist to identify the version of the drug available in Spain. Help and advice is available from the Overseas Section of the Department of Health (tel: 020 7210 4850).

If you are intending to retire to Spain, you should contact The Pension Service's International Pension Centre, which is part of the Department for Work and Pensions (tel: 0191 218 7777) or write to The International Pension Centre, at Newcastle Upon Tyne NE98 1BA. In Northern Ireland, you should contact the Northern Ireland Social Security Agency, International Services (24–42 Corporation Street, Belfast BT1 3DR; tel: 028 9054 3245). In either case, ask for copies of the various leaflets applicable.

Those living and working in Spain are generally required to join the Spanish social security system governing pensions, sickness, unemployment and healthcare. If you are employed, your employer is required to register you with the social security authorities and to deduct social security contributions from your salary. You should receive your social security card from your employer, to whom the authorities will send it. This is the proof of your entitlement, and the entitlement of your dependants, to medical cover, and will bear both your social security number and the name of the general practitioner to whom you will be initially assigned.

The self-employed are also required to make contributions, but the system is not identical to that applicable to salaried employees and you will need to check the up-to-date position. Medical and health care for your spouse and children are covered by your social security contributions.

If you are a UK national and have been sent to work in Spain by your employer, you should be entitled to cover under the Spanish health system while still paying your contributions to the UK system.

If you are in receipt of a UK state pension, you are entitled to treatment under the Spanish health system without contribution. You will need to obtain Form 121 to establish your entitlement. Spain has a considerable number of private hospitals and clinics, with a particularly heavy concentration in the Costa del Sol, where residents also have the possibility of choosing the British-run Westminster Private Medical Clinic in Gibraltar.

Private insurance

A number of Spanish and foreign companies offer health insurance cover, including *Sanitas*, used by many Spaniards. BUPA and Danmark As International Health Insurance are two other leaders in the field.

Language difficulties

Many Spanish doctors claim to speak English, but relatively few speak it to a high standard. Assistance is available from:

▌ the consulates of the various English-speaking nations that keep lists of English-speaking doctors;
▌ private health insurance and traveller's associations – these often provide details of English-speaking doctors to their clients;
▌ British and US hospitals based in Spain;
▌ the English-speaking press (see Appendix 1) may be able to provide you with details. On the Costa del Sol, for example, many doctors and other medical professionals advertise in *Sur in English*.

Pharmacies

As in many other countries, *farmacias* have a green neon light outside their premises. In Spain you can obtain a considerable number of products over the counter without a prescription, including antibiotics. However, unless you have a prescription you will pay in full even if you are registered with the state health service (with a prescription, the cost of medication is 100 per cent recoverable in connection with work-related accidents, and 60 per cent in other cases). The address of the duty out-of-hours pharmacist is posted in the windows of pharmacies, and can also be found in the local newspaper.

Emergency treatment

For medical (and indeed all) emergencies, you should phone 112. Those registered with the state health system do not pay for emergency ambulances, those who are privately insured will normally recover costs under their insurance policy. In addition, in most towns there are 24-hour private ambulance services. Private hospitals and clinics often have their own ambulances. Taxi drivers are legally obliged to take those in need of emergency treatment to hospital, if asked. They are entitled to payment. If you need to use a private vehicle to transport someone to hospital in an emergency, putting on the hazard lights and waving a white flag out of the window should make other drivers give you priority.

Emergency hospital care takes priority over means of payment, and so even if you are not able to prove that you have cover, or do not have cover, this is a matter for sorting out afterwards, and should not delay treatment.

Vaccinations

You are likely to be required to give details of vaccinations to your doctor, or your children's doctor, and indeed as a condition of school entry. The Spanish words for the diseases commonly vaccinated against are:

■ chickenpox – varicela
■ diphtheria – difteria
■ measles – sarampión
■ mumps – paperas
■ poliomyelitis – poliomielitis

- rubella – rubeola
- tetanus – tetanos
- tuberculosis – tuberculosis
- whooping cough – ferina *or* convulsiva

Working and setting up a business in Spain

Employment

Citizens of EU countries are entitled to live and work anywhere within the European Union. There are no formalities involved in going to search for employment in Spain, other than the possession of a valid passport. However, unemployment is high in Spain. Non-EU citizens will need to prove that they have a work contract, and that no competent Spanish person could be found to carry out the work.

Job seekers should register in person with their local office (*Oficina de Empleo*) of the *INEM* or *Instituto Nacional de Empleo* (Web site: www.inem.es). The larger offices may have a member of staff specializing in advising migrant workers seeking work within the European Union. Most offices will assist you in finding training courses, and advise on setting up your own business, as well as how best to obtain employment. You can also make contact with recruitment agencies by sending them a CV and covering letter requesting an appointment (see under *Trabajo tempora* in the *Yellow Pages*). Scan the classified ads under *Ofertas de Trabajo* (Job offers) in the main newspapers, including the English-language press, and also take a look at the job offers on the Web site of the British Chamber of Commerce in Spain: britishchamberspain.com. Finally, it can be worth sending unsolicited well-written letters and CVs to companies you are interested in. General help and guidance is available, including in English, on the government Web site: www.mtas.es

A covering letter must always be hand-written and in perfect Spanish. The CV should be very brief and to the point (one page only). The paper should be of good quality and the envelope should be white. Ideally, you should refer to one of the specialist books available on how to present different types of CVs and how to address and set out your correspondence.

There are many English speakers who are employed within the English community, particularly on the Costa del Sol and Costa Blanca, and speak hardly any Spanish, even after years of living in the country. On the Costa del Sol, numerous expatriates are in employment in the tourist industry, the yachting industry, security services, childcare and as domestic staff. Throughout Spain, there are a large number of English speakers who teach English as a foreign language having obtained a TEFL qualification in the UK, or teachers with PGCE (Post-Graduate Certificate in Education) who teach at one of the many UK or other international schools. However, while your chances of obtaining work will be increased by networking among other expatriates, or having a teaching qualification, if you are to obtain employment with a Spanish employer, a reasonable knowledge of Spanish and a willingness to improve it are essential.

Once you have obtained employment, your employer should register you with the social security authorities – it is illegal to work in Spain without being registered, and your employer can be fined upwards of 3,000 euros for failing to register you. You will need to apply for a *tarjeta comunitaria*, or permit, at the local *Delegado de Trabajo,* or a police station. You will need your contract of employment, passport, social security card, a medical certificate (which is available from a medical centre and simply states that you have no contagious diseases) and four passport-sized photographs. The authorities are obliged to grant these permits as of right to the citizen of any EU country. The permit is issued for one year, after which it should be renewed every five years. Along with the permit, you will be given a tax identification number.

Traditionally there has been an emphasis on employee rights, and job security, though following recent changes employers are increasingly offering mainly short-term contracts. Indeed, the European Economic and Social Committee of the European Union has called on Spain to reduce the number of temporary work contracts issued. The European Union has also asked Spain to increase the number of part-time contracts, which would go some way towards reducing the marked differences in unemployment between the sexes. Spain has a minimum wage, currently a little under 500 euros per month, with employees receiving roughly an extra month's salary in December and August (*pagas extraordinarias*). The average monthly salary is about 1,500 euros. The basic normal working week is 40 hours, and there is entitlement to one month's holiday in addition to 14 statutory holidays. Employees should be paid an additional 40 per cent for overtime, with double time on Sundays and statutory holidays. Most of an employee's social security contributions are paid by his or her employer. Working mothers with children under three receive a monthly benefit of 100 euros, a considerable help towards childcare costs.

The vast majority of employees in Spain do not need to complete a tax return, which is generally only required for those earning above a certain limit. Instead the authorities send employees an assessment of their tax liability each year, and their tax liability is then met by deductions made by their employers from their salaries, with any (usually minor) adjustments made at the end of April each year.

Starting and running a business in Spain

Setting up a new business in your home country is fraught with difficulties. Most new businesses fail in the first 12 months as a result of a variety of problems associated with inexperience, lack of planning, changing market conditions and plain bad luck. A major problem is lack of liquidity or cash flow, caused by overly optimistic sales forecasts and underestimating start-up costs.

Those seeking to set up business in Spain face additional hurdles:

▌ You will be are operating in a foreign land in which, to begin with at least, there will be more unknowns as a result of not being in your native surroundings. Furthermore, your business may not prosper unless it has a broad enough appeal to attract the local Spanish population, and/or other non-English speakers.

▌ To a greater or lesser extent, you will be operating in a foreign language. Even if your clientele is mainly English speaking, your suppliers may not be and your dealings with public officials and bodies will be in Spanish.

▌ Taken together the taxation and social security burden on businesses is higher than in the UK.

▌ Bureaucracy is acknowledged by the Spanish themselves to be very burdensome for businesses.

A substantial number of businesses rely on the expatriate British and other English-speaking communities, including bars, English bookshops, local newspapers, financial advisers, estate agents, suppliers of UK and US food and other produce, security and services relating to the yachting industry. Nevertheless, as a foreigner, you, or your business partner, will need to speak Spanish to a reasonable level or at least have a business adviser who is fluent in both languages. Your adviser must be familiar with matters of finance and have (not merely claim to have) substantial experience of advising businesses in Spain.

There are various agencies that provide help and assistance in establishing a business. Prior to leaving the UK, you could contact the Spanish Embassy (Commercial Office) at, 22 Manchester Square, London, W1M 5AP (tel: 020 7486 0101) and/or the Legal Department of the Spanish Embassy at 24 Belgrave Square, London, SW1X 8QA. A number of government booklets are available in English, including 'A Guide to Business in Spain', 'Forms of Business Organisations' and 'Labour Legislation.' Take a look at the British Chamber of Commerce in Spain Web site: britishchamberspain.com. The Chamber organizes seminars, conferences, discussions and workshops, and is a vital source of information and contacts for those carrying out business in Spain. The Chamber is based in Barcelona at Calle Bruc 21, 08010 Barcelona: tel 933 17 32 20 (e-mail enquiries to the director Sarah-Jane Stone britchamber@britchamber.com), but also has representation in Madrid, Bilbao and Zaragoza. Assistance can also be obtained from Barclays Bank www.barclays.es, or Lloyds TSB Bank www.lloydtsb.com. Barclays has branches in Madrid, Barcelona, Bilbao, Seville and Valencia, but following its recent acquisition of Banco Zaragozano, Barclays is set to treble its existing customer base and branch network in Spain. Lloyds TSB has branches in Madrid, Barcelona, the Canary Islands, Bilbao, Marbella, Majorca, Navarra and Seville.

Once in Spain, you should contact the local Spanish chamber of commerce. Ask what other help and assistance is available. In some areas, chambers of commerce run courses in English on how to set up a business.

According to a recent conference in Seville, the start-up costs for a small or medium-sized business in Spain amount to only 1,500 euros, far below the European average cost of 5,120 euros. Furthermore, the average time for the setting up of a business in Spain was one of the shortest, with an average of only 15 days being required. These figures, however, are averages and in reality, as a foreigner, you are likely to find that the costs and time required are greater, although with the correct professional advice you are likely to find it easier to set up business in Spain than, for example, in neighbouring France.

You should find a competent chartered accountant and/or commercial lawyer to advise on what form your business should take and assist with the necessary formalities. He or she can also advise you about the latest financial and other support available to businesses, and the various tax reliefs. It is vital that you choose someone with experience of doing business in Spain. See Appendix 1 for details of some practitioners. An essential source of help and advice, who will also save you time, is the *gestor* (see Chapter 9), who is well qualified to guide you through the bureaucratic nightmares and help with much of the paperwork that you will be required to complete. His or her charges will be relatively modest.

While any citizen of an EU country is entitled to live and work in Spain, a residence permit is not sufficient to enable you to start a business. A self-employed person, or *autónomo*, must also obtain a permit, as well as pay into the Spanish social security system, though on a different basis from an employee. A number of occupations – from doctor to hairdresser – are subject to specific restrictions and regulations, so you will need to make enquiries of the relevant professional body. It is fair to say, however, that foreign professionals now find it very much easier than in the past to have their qualifications recognized, and to establish themselves in Spain.

In order to establish yourself, you must obtain a form from the local police station or *Delegación de Trabajo*. To do this you will need:

▌ to take your certificates establishing your professional qualifications, your passport and a photocopy, four photographs and your lease or *escritura* for your business premises;

▌ to register at the *Hacienda* for payment of the *Impuesta de Actividades Economicas* (a licence, but in reality a tax on economic activity) – this tax is only payable when your turnover exceeds 600,000 euros, but you still need to register and obtain your code);

▌ to register at the local office of the social security authorities as a self-employed person. Monthly contributions start at a little over 200 euros;

▌ to obtain a licence for the opening of any business premises;

■ perhaps to produce other documentation (according to your individual circumstances); I would strongly advise that you instruct a *gestor* at the outset, as he or she is likely to save you a considerable amount of time and unnecessary stress.

The following vehicles are available for the running of a business:

■ You may operate as a sole trader. As in the UK, a sole trader is personally liable for the business's debts and losses.

■ You may operate in partnership. Again, partners remain personally liable.

■ You may run a limited liability company, or *Sociedad Limitada*. It is now possible for one person to form such a company. Should the business fail, the owners' liabilities are limited to the value of their shares in the company, but in practice it is likely that an owner is likely to have to give some personal guarantees, for example to the company's bank, or to its landlord if it operates from rented premises;

■ You may establish a *Sociedad Anónima* (SA). This is equivalent to a plc (public limited company) in the UK. Liability is limited to the amount of capital each investor puts into the company. Share capital of 60,000 euros is required.

■ You may run a branch of a foreign company.

Taxation of business

Social charges

If you are self-employed and do not employ anyone else, your social charges will cost at least 200 euros from the outset. Once you employ others, your social charges contributions will start to escalate. The employer's contributions are high. You should assume that once you have taken these into account and the additional two months' salary payable at Christmas and in the summer, the average total monthly cost of an employee will approach nearly twice his or her monthly salary. Remember that it is the employer's responsibility to register his or her employees, and that employers can be fined for failure to do this. Take advice on the type of contract to offer *before* employing anyone. Remember that it may not be easy to dismiss an employee without having to pay compensation.

Business taxes

The principles of corporate taxation in Spain are the same as in the rest of the European Union. The standard rate is 35 per cent, but 30 per cent for small and medium-sized businesses, and a large proportion of enterprises fit this category. Tax evasion is widespread, and major changes to the corporate tax system are expected.

When deciding on investing in the business by purchasing substantial assets, such as a computer system, you should note that not all the costs will be deductible against tax in the year in which they are purchased. The cost of such assets will be spread over a number of years and only a fraction will be deductible against tax in the year of purchase. You may wish to consider leasing equipment where tax deductions are more in line with your expenditure. You should, of course, keep records of your various expenses, in order to have these deducted against the business's revenue.

Business premises

As in the UK, a great deal of business property in Spain is leased. Like the residential tenant, the business tenant benefits from a degree of protection under the law, including a right to the renewal of his or her business lease. This right is subject to exceptions and the completion of the necessary formalities, and you should take advice from a lawyer and/or *gestor*. It is likely that the landlord will restrict the kind of business activity that may be operated from the premises. For any business premises you will also need a *licencia de apertura*, a licence permitting you to open your business. The cost of these varies, but it can be as little as 150 euros.

Bank finance

Having a business plan, in Spanish, is essential if you are to obtain a bank loan to finance your business. You will need to provide an assessment of the demand for your product or service, likely revenue, assets being introduced into the business, your fixed and variable costs and some cash flow forecasts. Banco Bilbao Vizcaya Argentaria (BBVA) has recently launched new fixed-rate loans for small and medium-sized businesses. As loans are at historic lows it is perhaps a good time for businesses to agree fixed rates to limit future financial costs.

State aid and other assistance

There are various subsidized loans, grants and subsidies available from the European Union, central, regional and local government, particularly in the less prosperous regions. In addition, there are several tax incentives and allowances in the early years of a business. Five companies have recently established a small and medium-sized businesses modernization programme. Spanish bank Bankinter, Spanish Informatica El Corte Inglés, the information technology subsidiary of Spanish retailer El Corte Inglés, US computer maker IBM, Spanish software developer SP and Spanish telecommunications company Telefónica have recently initiated a programme for promoting the use of high technologies in small and medium-sized enterprises in Spain. The initiative is aimed at companies with 1–250 employees and with an annual turnover of 40 million euros or less (95 per cent of all Spanish companies). The scheme provides software, hardware and telecommunications technologies.

Insurance

It is mandatory for businesses to have insurance cover for their vehicles, health insurance for their employees and property insurance. The notification period for claims is very short.

Spanish inheritance laws and the taxation of capital

When you purchase a property abroad, you *must* give consideration as to the effect that this is likely to have on the passing of your estate, and (if appropriate) how it will affect your spouse and children. In theory the situation is complex. Spanish law states that the disposal of a foreigner's property (even where the foreigner is resident in Spain) shall be in accordance with that person's own national law, i.e. UK law in the case of a UK citizen. The law of England and Wales, however, states that the passing of property should be in accordance with the rules of the country in which it is situated! While the 1989 Hague Convention provides that citizens of Europe can *choose* that the national laws of their home country should apply to their estate, the UK has not ratified the convention.

You really need to take legal advice from a lawyer with knowledge of the law in *both* your home country and Spain, and taking into account your particular circumstances and testamentary intentions.

Spanish rules of succession

These rules are important, because in Spain, as in other continental European countries, such as France, succession law restricts your freedom to dispose of your estate on your death. In brief, if your property is subject to Spanish succession rules, you are obliged to leave a proportion of your estate to your children, with some (rather limited) provision for your spouse. Accordingly, where a deceased has children, the *Ley de Herederos*

Forzosos stipulates that:

- a third must be left to the surviving children (or other issue) in equal shares;
- a second third must also be left to the children, although in relation to this third you may distribute this how you like amongst your issue, perhaps leaving it only to your grandchildren. This third, however, is subject to a life interest in favour of your surviving spouse, ie the spouse has the income from this third until his or her death;
- in relation to the last third, you retain complete control, and accordingly you may leave this third completely to your spouse.

Clearly, if a property (or other asset) is owned jointly, the surviving spouse will retain his or her half of the property, and the above inheritance rules will only apply to the share of the person who has died.

A working solution

It is currently common practice to make a Spanish will declaring that your national law provides for freedom of disposition of property on death, and to leave your Spanish property to the person you wish. The Spanish authorities have accepted this to date, and properties have simply been transferred into the names of the beneficiary stated in the will. What would happen, however, if a disinherited child wished to challenge the will, on the basis that part of the estate should have passed to him or her in accordance with Spanish law, remains to be seen.

While your UK will can be effective to pass property in Spain in accordance with UK rules of succession, the procedures are somewhat long-winded. Furthermore, a UK will may not have been drafted with Spanish inheritance tax in mind, and the consequences may be rather draconian for the beneficiaries of your estate.

Note that if you do not make a will, in practice your estate will be distributed in accordance with Spanish succession law for intestacy. This means that your estate will be divided equally between your children, though subject to a life interest in favour of your spouse – ie the spouse is entitled to the income from your estate, or, for example, can occupy the family home, until his or her death. As in the UK the estate of someone who dies intestate generally takes more time and expense to wind up.

Accordingly, you should seriously consider making a Spanish will, in addition to your UK will. The latter may well require updating to take account of your testamentary plans for your Spanish property. You should also note that if you emigrate to Spain, and have no remaining assets in the UK, your UK will may prove ineffective and fail to regulate the distribution of your entirely Spanish estate on your death.

Inheritance tax

Inheritance tax applies irrespective of whether your property is to be disposed of according to Spanish law, or the law of your home country. Your family will not be able to gain access to your Spanish estate until the tax is paid, and accordingly it is advisable to have a life policy that is sufficient to cover the tax that will be due, and indeed any outstanding mortgage. There is no exemption for a family home, and subject to a modest allowance, transfers on death to a spouse are taxed. All legacies under 16,000 euros are exempt, however, and accordingly no tax would be payable where a large estate is widely distributed. There are also exemptions of up to 48,000 euros for legacies passing to children, brothers, sisters and also spouses under the age of 21.

The amount of the tax is determined by three factors:

▌ the amount received by each beneficiary, and not by the size of the total estate;
▌ the relationship of the beneficiary to the deceased;
▌ the existing financial circumstances of the beneficiary.

The system of taxation is intended to encourage the passing of estates to close family members, with the lowest rates applicable to children, a spouse or parents and the highest rates to those to whom you are unrelated, including a common-law or same-sex partner. A common-law partner will pay tax at twice the rate of a married spouse. This does not apply in Andalusia, where the authorities now apply the same rules to unmarried as to married couples, and in some circumstances to same-sex couples.

As to the existing wealth of the beneficiaries, a recipient who has net assets above 400,000 euros pays a higher rate of tax.

The complexities are such that advice should be sought from an expert. There is double taxation relief, so that inheritance tax paid in Spain is taken into account in calculating liability for UK inheritance tax, and vice versa.

For residents of three years, there is a 95% exemption up to about 120,000 euros in relation to property left to a spouse or to children, or to a sibling of 65 years old who at the date of the death had been resident in the property for three years. In all cases the beneficiary must not sell the property for 10 years, or he or she will be liable to pay the tax that would have been due on the inheritance. In Andalusia this percentage has been increased to 99.9 per cent. Tax relief is available if you leave a business to your spouse or children.

The rates of tax for close family members rise to 34 per cent for amounts in excess of 800,000 euros. The tax-take on a taxable transfer (after exemptions) of 120,000 euros is about 15,600 euros, rising to 40,000 euros for a taxable transfer of 240,000 euros, 80,000 euros for a taxable transfer of 400,000 euros, and 200,000 euros on a taxable transfer of 800,000 euros. The marginal rates for a wealthy beneficiary who is not a close member of the deceased's family are 2.4 times higher, giving a marginal rate of 81.6 per cent for sums in excess of 800,000!

You should note that all property is taken into account, based on its market value at death. Personal effects in a home are valued at 3 per cent of the value of the home, but if they include items of substantial value such as antiques, it is likely that this rule will be disapplied. Life insurance is also included, with a modest exemption if it is in favour of a child. Payments on policies in favour of a spouse are in part taxed as income.

Avoiding Spanish inheritance tax

There are a number of ways open to you to lawfully reduce the liability of your successors to pay inheritance tax, including the creation of a family trust to own property. On the death of a member of the family, there is no transfer of ownership as the property remains vested in the trust and hence there is no liability to pay the tax. Another option is to sell your property to your heirs, but reserving the right to live in it for life. If you are a non-resident, you could consider purchasing your property via an offshore company. When you die the shares of the company will be disposed of according to the will you made in your own country, and there is no Spanish inheritance tax payable as there is no transfer of the Spanish property, which is still owned by the company. Off-shore companies owning property in Spain, however, are subject to an annual 3 per cent tax on the value of the property. If your estate is likely to be significant, you need to obtain expert tax advice at the outset.

Lifetime transfers are treated in the same way as transfers on death.

Making a will

You would be well advised to make a Spanish will dealing with land and property that you own in Spain if you are not resident there, or dealing with your entire estate if you are a Spanish resident. Reliance solely on your existing English will can have disastrous consequences, both in terms of inheritance rules and taxation. Your English will may need to be amended, for example to exclude your Spanish property.

By virtue of the Hague Convention of 1961, a will is valid if it is signed in accordance with the requirements either of the country in which it is signed or those of the testator's home country. Accordingly, an English person can sign a will in accordance with the formalities of English law – that is, that the will is signed in the presence of two witnesses, who each sign to have attested the will. A witness to a will cannot inherit under the will, nor can a member of his or her family.

You should keep a copy of your will and leave a copy with your lawyer or executor. The most recent will takes complete precedence over previous wills, provided that it indicates clearly that all previous wills are revoked.

Under no circumstances use a home-made will of the type that you can buy in the high street. Such wills are often unclear and are far more prone to result in protracted and expensive litigation than a will drafted by a competent lawyer.

Impuesto sobre el incremento patrimonial (capital gains tax)

Residents (generally those living in Spain for more than 183 days a year) pay a maximum rate of 15 per cent on capital gains. It is included in their income tax bill, and accordingly you do not have to declare the gain until the date for filing of the next income tax return. There are a number of exemptions, including the following:

▌ Residents over 65 are completely exempt from capital gains tax on their *principal* residence, providing they have lived in it for more than three years.
▌ The sale proceeds from the sale of a *principal* residence are completely exempt if used entirely to purchase another principal residence.
▌ A person who is over 65, and who sells his or her home in return for the right to live in it for life and receive an income is exempt from tax on any gain on the sale.
▌ Gains on property purchased prior to 1987 are not subject to the tax. Properties purchased after 1988 but before 31 December 1996 are subject to the tax, but there is sliding scale reduction. Both these provisions apply to residents and non-residents alike.

Both residents and non-residents can set off their costs of purchase against the tax, and both benefit from an annual inflation allowance that is applied to the purchase price and reduces the gain. Non-residents pay a uniform rate of 35 per cent, and the tax should be declared within a short time of the sale. In relation to sales of property, the vendor will, of course, retain 5 per cent of the sale proceeds that he or she pays to the tax authorities on account of the tax. Non-residents, including UK residents, may be liable in their home country for the gain on their Spanish property. Fortunately a double taxation agreement with Spain means that you will not have to pay the full tax twice.

Impuesto sobre el patrimonio (wealth tax)

Both residents and non-residents are required to pay a tax on their capital assets. If you are resident, the tax is based on the *market* value of *all* your *worldwide* assets. That means anything and everything of value, save for reasonable home furnishings. Mortgages and other debts are deducted from the total value of your assets, as is any similar tax that you are required to pay abroad. There is an exemption of 150,000 euros per person for one's principal residence. Accordingly, a couple with a property valued at 350,000 with a mortgage of 100,000 and other assets totalling 50,000 euros would not pay tax.

The tax rate on the first 170,000 euros or so is 0.2 per cent, rising to a marginal rate of 2.5 per cent for those with assets over 10.7 million euros. The following table gives examples of the approximate wealth tax bill to be paid by a couple.

Net assets (euros)	Approximate annual tax (euros)
640,000	650
1,000,000	1700
2,000,000	7,500

The wealth tax declaration must be made at the same time as the income tax declaration.

Not surprisingly, a non-resident is only required to include his or her assets in Spain, but clearly there can be no principal residence exemption. Non-residents must make annual declarations.

In recent years the autonomous regions, including Andalusia and the Canary Islands, have been given the right to fix their own rates of wealth tax, and accordingly rates may well vary depending on your region.

Imputed income tax

The Spanish tax authorities impute an income to your property (other than your principal residence, which is exempt) generally calculated at 2 per cent of the *valor catastral*. The sum is included as income in your income tax declaration, and then taxed at the individual's rate of taxation. For non-residents the tax is fixed at 25 per cent, making a tax of 0.5 per cent of the *catastral* value.

Appendix 1: Useful addresses

See also regional information in Chapter 2.

British Embassy and consulates

British Embassy
C/de Fernando el Santo 16, 28010 Madrid
Tel: 913 19 02 00
e-mail: presslibrary@ukinspain.com
www.ukinspain.com The Web site contains a considerable deal of useful information on a wide range of subjects.

Alicante
British Consulate, Plaza Calvo Sotelo 1–2, 03001 Alicante
Tel: 965 21 61 90
e-mail: enquries.alicante@fco.gov.uk

Barcelona
British Consulate General, Avenida Diagonal 477–13, 08036 Barcelona
Tel: 933 66 62 00

Bilbao
British Consulate General, Alamada de Urquijo 2–8, 48008 Bilbao
Tel: 944 15 76 00

Madrid
British Consulate General, Centro Colon, Marques de la Ensenada 16, 28004 Madrid
Tel: 913 08 52 01

Malaga
British Consulate, Edificio Duquesa, Duquesa de Parcent 8, 29001 Malaga
Tel: 952 352 300
e-mail: malaga@fco.gov.uk

Palma de Majorca
British Consulate, Plaza Mayor 3D, 07002 Palma de Majorca
Tel: 971 36 33 73
e-mail: consulate@palma.mail.fco.gov.uk

Las Palmas
British Consulate, Edificio Cataluna, Luis Morote 6–3, 35007 Las Palmas
Tel: 928 26 25 08

Santa Cruz de Tenerife
British Consulate, Plaza Weyler 8–1, 38003 Santa Cruz de Tenerife
Tel: 922 28 68 63

Santander
Honorary British Consulate, Paseo de Pereda 27, 39004 Santander
Tel: 942 22 00 00

Other embassies

Australia
Pasco de la Castellana 143, 28046 Madrid
Tel: 915 79 04 28

Canada
C/Nunez de Balboa 35, 28001 Madrid
Tel: 914 31 43 00

Denmark
C/Claudio Coello 91, 28006 Madrid
Tel: 914 31 84 45

Germany
C/Fortuny 8, 28010 Madrid
Tel: 913 19 63 10

Ireland
C/Claudio Coello, 73, 28001 Madrid
Tel: 915 76 35 09

Netherlands
Avda. Del Comandante Franco 32, 28016 Madrid
Tel: 913 59 09 14

New Zealand
Plza. de la Lealtad 2, 28014 Madrid
Tel: 915 10 31 16

Norway
Paeso de la Castellana, 31, 28046 Madrid
Tel: 913 10 31 16

South Africa
C/Claudio Coello 91, 28006 Madrid
Tel: 914 35 66 88

Sweden
C/Caracas 25, 28010 Madrid
Tel: 913 08 15 35

United States of America
C/Serrano, 75, 28006 Madrid
Tel: 915 77 40 00

Spanish Embassies and Consulates

UK

The Spanish Embassy, 39 Chesham Place, London SW1X 8SB
Tel: 020 7235 555
e-mail: embespuk@mail.mae.es

General information on Spain.

The Spanish Consulate General, 20 Draycott Place, London SW3 2RZ
Tel: 020 7898 989
e-mail: consplon@mail.mae.es

The Spanish Consulate Manchester, Suite 1A, Brookhouse, 70 Spring
Gardens, Manchester M2 2BQ
Tel: 061 236 1262
e-mail: conspmanchester@mail.mae.es

The Spanish Consulate Edinburgh, 63 North Castle Street, Edinburgh
EH2 3LI
Tel: 0131 220 1843
e-mail: cgspedimburgo@mail.mae.es

United States

The Spanish Embassy, 2375 Pennsylvania Avenue, NW, Washington DC
20037
Tel: 202 452 0100

Canada

The Spanish Embassy, 74 Stanley Avenue, Ottawa, Ontario K1M 1P4
Tel: 613 747 2252

Spanish Tourist Offices

UK

22–23, Manchester Square, London W1M 5AP
Tel: 020 7486 8077
www.tourspain.co.uk

United States

666 Fifth Avenue, New York, NY 10103
Tel: 212 265 8822
8383 Wilshire Bd, Suite 960, Beverly Hills, CA 90211
Tel: 323 658 7188

Canada

2 Bloor Street West, 34th Floor, Toronto, Ontario M4W 3E2
Tel: 416 961 3131
Web site: www.tourspain.toronto.on.ca

The British Council

Plaza Santa Barbara 10, 28010 Madrid
Tel: 913 191 250
Web site: www.britishcouncil.co.uk/
Information on education and equivalence of qualifications.

British Chambers of Commerce in Spain

Barcelona
Calle Bruc 21, 1º 4ª 08010 Barcelona
Tel: 933 17 32 20
Fax: 933 02 48 96
e-mail: britchamber@britchamber.com
Director: Sarah-Jane Stone

Madrid
Roger Fry, OBE, Maestro Lassalle 46, 28016 Madrid
Tel: 913 45 63 44
Fax: 913 59 27 67
e-mail: moreno@kingsgroup.com

Bilbao
British Chamber of Commerce Association en Bilbao
Ercilla 24, 2º dpto 19, 48011 Bilbao
Tel: 944 15 93 99
Fax: 944 79 09 22

Aragon
Graham Rhodes
Pl. del Carmen 1, 1ª 50004 Zaragoza
Tel: 976 22 93 14
Fax: 976 22 93 14
e-mail: grahamis@teleline.es

Banks

Barclays Bank
www.barclays.es

Madrid
Plaza de Colón 1, 28046 Madrid
Tel: 913 36 13 15/10 00
Fax: 913 36 12 22

Barcelona
Paseo de Gracia 45, 08007 Barcelona
Tel: 934 81 20 00
Fax: 932 15 85 72

Bilbao
Alameda de Recalde 36, 48009 Bilbao
Tel: 944 23 64 86
Fax: 944 24 44 21

Seville
Tetuán 32, 41001 Sevilla Tel: 954 22 09 90
Fax: 954 21 26 45

Valencia
Barcas 4, 46002 Valencia
Tel: 963 52 30 85
Fax: 963 51 17 81

Lloyds TSB
www.lloydstsb.es

Madrid
Serrano, 90, 28006 Madrid
Tel: 915 20 99 00
Fax: 915 77 28 10

Barcelona
Calvet, 16–22, 08021 Barcelona
Tel: 933 62 45 10
Fax: 933 62 45 14

Bilbao
Gran Vía 64, 48011
Tel: 944 39 31 12
Fax: 944 41 28 53

Canary Islands
Avda de Anaga, 37–39, 38001 Islas Canarias Santa Cruz de Tenerife
Tel: 922 53 36 00
Fax: 922 28 39 16

Majorca
Paseo de la Mallorca 4, 07012 Palma de Mallorca
Tel: 971 21 37 90

Navarra
Avda Roncesvalles 11, Pamplona, 31002 Navarra
Tel: 948 20 69 70

Seville
Plaza Nueva 8, 41001 Sevilla
Tel: 954 50 15 46

Business

British Chamber of Commerce in Spain (see above).

Commercial lawyers

Monero, Meyer & Marinel-lo Abogados S.L, Pg. de Gràcia 98, 4⁰ 2ª, 08008
Barcelona (with offices in Madrid and Majorca)
Tel: 934 87 58 94
Fax: 934 87 38 44
www.mmmm.es

Accountants

Ernst & Young
S.L. Avenida Diagonal 575 (L'Illa), 08029 Barcelona
Tel: 933 66 37 00/38 00
Fax: 934 05 37 84 www.ey.com/es

Churches

A comprehensive list of Anglican churches throughout Spain can be
accessed from www.anglican-mallorca.org; go to 'dioceses in Europe' at
the foot of the home page, and then to 'location'.

An extensive list of English-speaking churches on the Costa del Sol
(including Anglican/Episcopal, Roman Catholic, Presbyterian, Methodist
and Evangelical and non-denominational) is to be found on the Web site
www.surinenglish.com, which also has details of mosques.

English bookshops

The Shakespeare Second Hand Bookshop
Calle Lagasca, 69 San Pedro de Alcantara, Costa del Sol

Bookworld Espana
Las Palmeras 25, San Pedro Alcantara
Tel: 952 78 63 66

Avda Jesus Santos Rein, Fuengirola
Tel: 952 66 48 37

English-language newspapers and journals

Absolute Marbella
Office 21, Edificio Tembo, C/Rotary International s/n, Puerto Banus, Marbella
Tel: 952 90 86 17
E-mail: info@absolute-marbella.com
www.absolute-marbella.com

Costa del Sol News
Apartado 102, 29630 Benalmadena Costa, Malaga
Tel: 952 44 92 50
e-mail: costasol@dragonet.es

Costa Blanca News
Apartado 95, 03500 Benidorm, Alicante
Tel: 966 81 28 41
Web site: www.costablanca-news.com

The Island Gazette
C/Iriate 43–2, Puerto de la Santa Cruz, Tenerife

The Majorca Daily Bulletin
Sam Feliu, 25, Palma de Mallorca, Mallorca
Tel: 971 78 84 00
Web site: www.majorcadailybulletin.es

Sur in English
Avenida Doctor Maraiton 48, 290009, Malaga
Tel: 952 64 96 00
www.surinenglish.com

See also www.spainview.com

Estate agents

Numerous estate agents have Web sites that are easily accessible, including via a number of information Web sites, as listed below.

Spanish Property Centre
2 Alva Street, Edinburgh
Tel: 0131 226 6633

Anglo Continental Properties
Tel: 01926 401274
www.anglocontinental.co.uk

Guide to Timeshares
www.guidetotimeshares.com

Taylor Woodrow
www.taywoodspain.co.uk

www.123propertynews.com

www.andalucia.com

www.apartmentspain.co.uk

www.buyspanish.co.uk

www.hiddenspain.co.uk

www.marbella-lawyers.com

www.propertyfinance4less.com

www.spanishproperty.com

www.worldclasshomes.co.uk

Expatriate Web sites

There are very many such sites, some of which are listed (with links) at the Back in Blighty Web site under 'Expat Links' (see www.backinblighty.com/).

Financial advice

Blevins Franks International
Barbican House, 26–34 Old Street, London EC1 9QQ
Tel: 0207 336 1022
In Spain, tel: 952 79 97 52
e-mail: infolondon@blevinsfranks.com
www.blevinsfranks.com

Siddalls International
Tel: 01329 288641
e-mail: investment@johnsiddals.co.uk

Information

Many of the sites listed in this Appendix, such as those of the British Embassy in Madrid, and the Spanish Embassy in London, contain information on Spain. See also www.surinenglish.com (for information on the Costa del Sol).

Legal contacts

UK

Baily Gibson, 5 Station Parade, Beaconsfield, Bucks HP29 2PG
Tel (UK): 01494 672661
Fax (UK): 01494 678493
DX: 34500 Beaconsfield
e-mail: susanad@bailygibson.co.uk or Susanan@bailygibson.co.uk

Michael Soul & Associates, 16 Old Bailey, London EC4M 7EG
Tel: 0207 597 6292
e-mail: mailbox@spanishlawyers.co.uk
www.spanishlawyers.co.uk
Also offices in Marbella and Madrid

Bennett & Co, 144 Knutsford Road, Wilmslow, Cheshire SK9 6JP, UK
Tel: +44 (0) 1625 586937
Fax: +44 (0) 1625 585362
e-mail: internationallawyers@bennett-and-co.com
www.bennett-and-co.com
Contact: Trevor Bennett or Trish Fletcher

Lawyers4Spanish-Homes

UK: Equity House, Blackbrook Park Avenue, Taunton TA1 2PX
Tel: 0845 083 3000 (24/7)
Fax: 0845 083 3001
Contact: Stephen Ward

Gibraltar: Suites 15 & 17, First Floor, Watergardens 3, Waterport, PO Box 883, Gibraltar
Tel: 00 350 43754 (from Spain: 9567 43754)
Fax: 00 350 76553 (from Spain: 9567 76553)
e-mail: info@Lawyers4Spanish-Homes.com
www.Lawyers4Spanish-Homes.com
Contact: Nick Cruz

All about Spain Ltd, 104 The Corn Exchange, Fenwick Street, Liverpool L2 7QL
Tel: 0870 33 09 131
Fax: 0870 33 09 132
www.allaboutspain.co.uk

Edgar Wagner: Anglo-Spanish Law, 6 Lower Burch Row, Eyam, Hope Valley, Sheffield S32 5QF
Tel: 01433 631 508
e-mail: anglospanishlaw@legalisp.net

J Palanco Abad & Associados, Heal House, 375 Kennington Lane, London SE11 5QY
Tel: 0207 793 8800
e-mail: demigpol@aol.com

Spain

Costa del Sol: Esther Wilkie, Plaza Abogados, Puerto Sotogrande, Edificio C Puerta 2, 11310 Sotogrande
Tel: 956 79 02 80

Carlos Llanos & Francisco Dopico, Plaza Abogados, Edificio Puerta del Mar, Oficina B1, TVA de Carlos Mackintosh s/n, Marbella, Malaga
Tel: 952 82 93 93

Domingo Cuadra, Calle Calvario 8, Edificio Marbelsun 1–1–10, 29600 Marbella
Tel: 952 82 91 44

Costa Brava: Aurelia Fortuny, De Fortuny Abogados, Calle Aragon no. 235 Pral. 2a ESC.DCHA, 08007 Barcelona
Tel: 934 87 26 79

Almeira: Michael John Davies, Parque Comercial 50, Mojacar, Almeira
Tel: 950 47 27 75

Canary Islands: Santiago Martin Helva, Apartado de Correos 105, Los Cristianos, Arona 386400 Tenerife
Tel: 922 75 23 43

Balearic Islands: Caballero Lafuente Mercadal Abogados Asociados, Calle Norte 12, Mahon, Menorca
Tel: 971 35 25 72

Removal firms

Allied Pickfords
Tel: 0800 289 229

Bishop's Move
Tel: 0800 616 425
www.bishopsmove.com

Britannia Bradshaw International
Tel: 0161 946 0809
www.bradshawinternational.com

Overs International
Tel: 0800 243433
www.overs.co.uk

World Wide Shipping & Airfreight Co.
Tel: 02380 633 660
www.worldfreight.co.uk

Schools

See the Web site of the British Council: www.britishcouncil.co.uk. Click on 'Education' for details of the Spanish education system. See also other addresses and Web sites referred to in Chapter 11.

Spanish – learning the language

Instituto Cervantes
102 Eaton Square, London SW1W 9AN
Tel: 0207 235 0353/0329
www.cervantes.es
e-mail: cenlon@cervantes.es

326–330 Deansgate, Campfield Avn. Arcade, Manchester M3 4FN
Tel: 0161 661 4200/4203
e-mail: cenman@cervantes.es

58, Northumberland Road, Ballsbridge, Dublin 4
Tel: 35 31 668 29 36/35 31 668 84 16
e-mail: cendub@cervantes.es

First established in 1991, Instituto Cervantes now has over 40 centres worldwide, including in New York, Chicago and Albuquerque in the United States. A full list can be seen on the Web site www.cervantes.es by clicking on 'IC en el mundo'. At the time of writing there were no centres in Canada, Australia, New Zealand, South Africa or any of the Scandinavian countries.

Europa Pages
www.europa-pages.co.uk/spain/
A directory of schools, colleges and universities offering Spanish language tuition in Spain.

People Going Global
www.peoplegoingglobal.com
A directory of universities and other establishments where one can study Spanish in Spain, and access to the Newcomers Club Directory for Spain.

Surveyors

Geoffrey Fielding
The Fielding Partnership, La Carolina, Edificio Aries Local 36A, Crta. De Cadiz KM 178.5, Marbella, Malaga
Tel: 952 82 67 54

Geoff Campion
The Fielding Partnership, Apartado 65, 07400 Alcudia, Mallorca
Tel: 971 89 16 14

Mike Woodhouse
38 Parque Albatros, Costa del Silencio, Arona, Tenerife
Tel: 922 73 05 74

Transport

Airlines

British Airways
Tel: 0845 773 3377
www.britishairways.com

BMI Baby
Tel: 0870 607 0555
www.flybmi.com

easyJet
Tel: 0870 600 0000
www.easyjet.co.uk

GB Airways
Tel: 0870 850 9850
www: gbairways.com

Iberia
www.iberia.com

Jet 2
Tel: 0870 737 8282
www.jet2.com

Ryanair
Tel: 0871 246 0000
Web site: www.ryanair.com

The Web site for British Airways Authority is www.baa.co.uk (links to Aberdeen, Edinburgh, Glasgow, London Gatwick, London Heathrow and Southampton airports). See also www.cheap-flights-to-spain.co.uk Tel: 0870 990 8009.

Ferries

Brittany Ferries
Tel: 0870 556 1600
www.brittany-ferries.com

Condor
Tel: 0845 345 2000
www.condorferries.co.uk

Hoverspeed
Tel: 0870 240 8070
www.hoverspeed.com

Irish Ferries
Tel: 0870 517 1717
www.irishferries.com/

Norfolkline
Tel: 0870 870 1020
www.norfolkline.com

P&O Ferries
Tel: 0870 600 0611
www.poferries.com

P&O Portsmouth
Tel: 0870 242 4999
www.poportsmouth.com

SeaFrance
Tel: 0870 571 1711
www.seafrance.com

Transmanche
Tel: 0800 9171201
www.transmancheferries.com

Rail

Eurotunnel
Tel: 0870 535 3535
www.eurotunnel.com

French Motorail
Tel: 0870 241 5415
www.frenchmotorail.com

Spanish National Railways
Tel: 902 240 202
www.renfe.es

Rail Europe
Tel: 0870 584 8848
www.raileurope.co.uk

Road and route planning

AA
www.theaa.com

Mappy
www.mappy.com

RAC
www.rac.co.uk

Appendix 2:
Direct flights to Spain from the UK and Ireland

THE AIRPORTS OF MAINLAND SPAIN

The details given below will obviously be subject to change and should be checked with the operator concerned.

MAINLAND SPAIN

To	From	Airline
Alicante	Bristol	easyJet
	Cardiff	BMI Baby
	Cork	Aer Lingus
	Dublin	Aer Lingus
	East Midlands	easyJet, BMI Baby
	Exeter	Flybe
	Leeds/Bradford	Jet2
	Liverpool	easyJet
	London Gatwick	easyJet, BA, GB Airways, Iberia
	London Luton	easyJet, Monarch
	London Stansted	easyJet
	Manchester	Monarch, BMI Baby
	Newcastle	easyJet
	Southampton	Flybe
	Teesside	Flybe
Almeira	London Gatwick	GB Airways
Barcelona	Birmingham	BA, Iberia, Ryanair
	Bournemouth	Ryanair
	Bristol	easyJet
	Cork	Aer Lingus
	Dublin	Aer Lingus, Iberia, Ryanair
	East Midlands	BMI Baby, easyJet
	Glasgow	BA, Ryanair
	Leeds/Bradford	Jet2
	Liverpool	easyJet
	London Gatwick	easyJet, BA,
	London Heathrow	Iberia
	London Luton	easyJet
	London Stansted	easyJet, Ryanair
	Manchester	Iberia, BMI Baby
	Newcastle	easyJet

Appendix 2: Direct Flights from the UK and Ireland

To	From	Airline
Bilbao	London Gatwick	easyJet
	London Heathrow	Iberia
	London Stansted	easyJet
Jerez de la Frontera	London Stansted	Ryanair
Madrid	Birmingham	BA
	Dublin	Aer Lingus
	Liverpool	easyJet
	London Gatwick	easyJet
	London Heathrow	BA, British Midland, Iberia
	London Luton	easyJet
Malaga	Bristol	easyJet
	Cardiff	BMI Baby
	Cork	Aer Lingus
	Coventry	Thomsonfly
	Dublin	Aer Lingus, Ryanair
	East Midlands	easyJet, BMI Baby
	Exeter	Flybe
	Leeds/Bradford	Jet 2
	Liverpool	easyJet
	London Gatwick	easyJet, GB Airways, Monarch
	London Heathrow	GB Airways, Iberia
	London Luton	easyJet, Monarch
	London Stansted	easyJet
	Manchester	Monarch, BMI Baby
	Southampton	Flybe
	Teesside	Flybe
Murcia	Birmingham	Ryanair
	East Midlands	BMI Baby
	Leeds/Bradford	Jet 2
	London Gatwick	BA, GB Airlines
	London Stansted	Ryanair
	Manchester	BMI Baby
	Southampton	Flybe
Santiago de Compostela	London Heathrow	Iberia

To	From	Airline
Seville	London Gatwick	GB Airways
Valencia	London Heathrow	GB Airways
	Coventry	Thomsonfly
Valladolid	London Stansted	Ryanair
CANARY ISLANDS		
Gran Canaria	London Gatwick	GB Airways
Tenerife	London Gatwick	GB Airways, Iberia
	Luton	Monarch
	Manchester	Monarch
BALEARIC ISLANDS		
Ibiza	East Midlands	BMI Baby
	London Stansted	easyJet
	Coventry	Thomsonfly
	Manchester	BMI Baby
Menorca	Luton	Monarch
	London Gatwick	GB Airways
Palma	Bristol	easyJet
	Cardiff	BMI Baby
	Coventry	Thomsonfly
	East Midlands	BMI Baby
	Leeds/Bradford	Jet2
	Liverpool	easyJet
	London Gatwick	easyJet, Monarch, GB Airways, Iberia
	London Heathrow	British Midland
	London Luton	easyJet
	London Stansted	easyJet
	Manchester	Monarch, BMI Baby
	Teesside	Flybe
GIBRALTAR		
	London Gatwick	GB Airways
	London Heathrow	GB Airways
	Luton	Monarch
	Manchester	Monarch

Appendix 2: Direct Flights from the UK and Ireland

To	From	Airline
PORTUGAL		
Faro	Bristol	easyJet
	Dublin	Ryanair
	Leeds/Bradford	Jet2
	East Midlands	easyJet, BMI Baby
	Exeter	Flybe
	London Luton	easyJet, Monarch
	London Stansted	easyJet
	Manchester	Monarch
FRANCE		
Biarritz	London Stansted	Ryanair
Perpignan	London Stansted	Ryanair
	Southampton	Flybe
	Birmingham	Flybe

Note that Iberia Airlines flies to all main Spanish locations, and operates from Aberdeen, Birmingham, Cork, Dublin, Edinburgh, Glasgow, Manchester, Newcastle and Shannon, often with changes at London. See www.iberia.com

Details of airline telephone numbers and Web sites can be found in Appendix 1.

Appendix 3:
Useful Spanish words and phrases

Conveyancing and legal terminology

abogado	lawyer, solicitor
agente de la propriedad inmobiliara	estate agent
administrador de fincas	a licensed property manager
arras	deposit paid on a contract
arrendamiento	sitting tenant
cargos	charges
catastro	land registry
certificado	certificate
certificado de fin de obra	certificate from builder or architect on completion of works
certificado de matrimonio	marriage certificate
ciudadania	citizenship
clausula condicional	conditional clause in contract
complejo residencial	housing complex
comprar	to purchase
comprador	purchaser
comprar al contado	to pay cash
comprar sobre plano	to purchase a property before it is built
compraventa	buying and selling
contable	accountant
contrato	contract

contrato de arrendamiento/alquiler	rental agreement
contrato de compraventa	sales contract
contrato de opción de compra	option to buy
contrayente	contracting party
cosas comunes	common parts (of a block of flats)
demandar	to sue
desocupado	vacant
embargo	a charge registered against a property for any unpaid debts
estado de cuenta	bank statement
escritura	deed of sale
firma	signature
garantizar	to guarantee
gestor	licensed professional who acts for individuals in their dealings with the state
hipoteca	mortgage
honorarios	fees
impuesto sobre actos juridicos documentados	stamp duty on transfer of property
llave	key
llave en mano	ready for immediate occupation
ley	a law
mudanza	removal
multa	fine, penalty
notario	public notary who oversees property transactions
parcello	building plot
permiso de obra	planning permission
persianas	blinds
piedra	stone
pintoresco	picturesque
pintura	paintwork
piscina	swimming pool
planta	floor, storey
planta baja	ground floor
poder	Power of Attorney
postigo	shutter

pozo	well
pozo negro	cesspit
precio	price
prestamo	loan
presupuesto	estimate/quote
promotor	developer
puerta	door
radiodores	radiator
reformar	to refurbish
reparación	repair
en ruinos	in ruins
sala de estar	sitting room
salón	living room
sanción	penalty, fine
seguro decenal	10-year structural insurance
sótano	basement
subasta	auction
taladradora	drill
talle	workshop
techo	ceiling
tejado	roof
trastero	storage room
trozo	length (of pipe or wood)
urbanización	purpose-built housing development
usufructo	life interest
valor catastral	value of property for official or tax purposes
valorar	to value
vendedor	seller
vista	view
vivienda secundaria	second home

Types of property

adosado	semi-detached, often in modern developments
apartamento/piso	apartment
apartamento de lujo	exclusive apartment
apartamento de vacaciones	holiday apartment
apartamento duplex	duplex apartment
buhardilla	top-floor flat under eaves
casa	house, home
casa de epoca	old house, period home
casa rural	rural home
casa señorial	exclusive property
casa urbana	urban home
caserio	country house
chalet	detached villa, house
chalet semi-adosado	semi-detached house
complejo residencial	residential complex
cortijo	country house/farm house
estudio	studio flat
finca	estate or farm (including its land)
finca urbana	urban estate
granja	farm
llave en mano	ready for immediate occupation
masia	type of farmhouse in Catalonia
multipropiedad	timeshare
piso	apartment, flat
rascacielos	skyscraper
solar	building plot
ultimo piso	top floor

Property descriptions, condition of the property and estate agents

accesorios	fittings
aire acondicionado	air conditioning
alfombra	carpet
alicatado	tiling (walls)
amiante	asbestos
anexos	building extensions
antena	aerial
aparcamiento	car park
árboles	trees
arquitecto	architect
arroyo	stream
ascensor	lift/elevator
azota	flat roof
azulejos	tiles
balcon	balcony
banera	bath
barrio	neighbourhood/suburb
barro cocido	terracotta
basura	rubbish, garbage
bien situado	good location
bodega	cellar (for storage or wine)
bombona	gas bottle
bosque	woods/forest
bricolage	DIY
caldera	water heater, boiler
calefacción	heating
calefacción general	common heating system
calle (c/)	street
canaleta	gutter (on roof)
carpintero	carpenter
cesped	lawn
cielo	ceiling
clavo	nail
cocina	kitchen (or cooker)

cocina americana	fitted kitchen
cocina comedor	kitchen-diner
comedor	dining room
construcción	building
constructor	builder
cuarto	room
cuarto de baño	bathroom
dependencia	outbuildings
deposito de agua	water tank
desván/altillo	attic/loft
dintel	lintel
dirección	address
doble cristal	double-glazing
dormitorio	bedroom
ducha	shower
edificio	building
electrodomésticos	domestic appliances
enchufe	electric socket
entrado	entrance
escalara	ladder
estante	shelf
establo	stable
estado	condition, state
estancia	room
estructura	structure
fosa séptica	septic tank
fontaneria	plumbing
garaje	garage
garantizar	to guarantee
granero	barn
grava	gravel
habitable	habitable
hormgon	concrete
humedad	dampness
impermeable	waterproof
inspección	survey
instalación de agua	plumbing
interruptor	switch

ladrillo	brick
lavabo	washbasin
leña	firewood
llave	tap
mantenimiento	maintenance
martillo	hammer
membrana aislante	damp course
metros cuadrados	square metres
mobiliario	fixed furnishings
moquetta	fitted carpet
obra	work, construction
ocasión	bargain
parabólica	satellite dish
pared de cargo	supporting wall
pestillo	bolt
suministro de agua	water supply
suministro de electricidad	electricity supply

Renting

alquilar	to rent
se alquila	for rent
amueblado	furnished
apartamento amueblado	furnished apartment
arrendamiento	rent
casa preaviso	notice
casero	landlord
contrato de arrendamiento	lease
fianza	deposit on renting
inquilino	tenant

Utilities

abono	standing charge
contador	meter

Financial

asegurar	to insure
banco	bank
cuenta corriente	current account
derecho	a right
entidad	lender
gastos	expenses
gastos excluidos	utility bills
impuesto sobre bienes inmuebles (IBI)	property tax
impuesto sobre el Patrimonia	wealth tax
pagar a plazos	to pay by instalments
prestamo	loan
recibo	receipt
seguro de hogar	household insurance
tipos de interes	interest rate

Dealing with the authorities

ciudadania	citizenship
comisario	police station
matricula	registration (eg car)
municipalidad	town hall
pais de origen	native country
permiso de residencia	residence permit

Miscellaneous

farmaceutico	pharmacist
gas	gas
interior	hinterland
médico de médicina general	GP
plomo	fuse
receta	prescription

Internet

abrir	to open
arroba	@
ayuda	help
barra de herramientas	tool bar
buscador	search engine
cerrar	to exit
copiar	to copy
datos adjuntos	attachment
dirección de correo electronico	e-mail address
eliminar	to delete
guardar como	to save as
guión	hyphen
imprimar	to print
en linea	on line
pantalla	screen
punto com	dot com
sitios web	Web site
transvaar	to download
uve doble, uve doble, uve doble	www

Appendix 4:
Pet travel scheme – approved routes and carriers to Spain

By sea

Santander to Portsmouth	Brittany Ferries (winter only)
Santander to Plymouth	Brittany Ferries (summer only)

By air

Spain

Alicante	London Gatwick	Britannia Airways, GB Airways, Monarch Airlines
	London Heathrow	bmi british midland
Almeria	London Gatwick	GB Airways
Arrecife	London Gatwick	Britannia Airways
Barcelona	London Gatwick	British Airways
	London Heathrow	KLM Cargo (via Amsterdam)
Fuerteventura	London Gatwick	Britannia Airways
Girona	London Gatwick	GB Airways
Ibiza	London Gatwick	Britannia Airways
Lanzarote	London Gatwick	GB Airways
Las Palmas	London Gatwick	Britannia Airways
Madrid	London Heathrow	bmi british midland, KLM Cargo (via Amsterdam)

Mahon	London Gatwick	Britannia Airways, GB Airways
Malaga	London Gatwick	Britannia Airways, GB Airways, Monarch Airlines
	London Heathrow	GB Airways
Murcia	London Gatwick	GB Airways
Palma, Majorca	London Gatwick	GB Airways, Britannia Airways
	London Heathrow	bmi british midland
Seville	London Gatwick	GB Airways
Tenerife North, Canary Islands	London Gatwick	GB Airways
	London Heathrow	bmi british midland
Tenerife South, Canary Islands	London Gatwick	Britannia Airways, GB Airways
	London Heathrow	bmi british midland
Valencia	London Gatwick	GB Airways

Portugal

Faro	London Gatwick	Britannia Airways, GB Airways, Monarch Airlines

Gibraltar

Gibraltar	London Gatwick	GB Airways

The above information is subject to variation, so you should check before making your travel plans. Pets travel as cargo, though on a small number of flights guide dogs are permitted in the cabin. See the DEFRA Web site (details below).

Information

Pets helpline
Tel: 0870 241 1710 (Monday–Friday, 8.30 am to 5.00 pm, UK time)
www.defra.gov.uk
e-mail: helpline@defra.gsi.gov.uk

Appendix 5:
Public holidays

1 January	New Year's Day (*Año Nuevo*)
6 January	Epiphany (*Reyes Magos*)
19 March	San Jose (*Dia de San José*)
Easter Easter Monday	*Semana Santa*
1 May	Labour Day
Pentecost	Second Monday after Ascension
May/June	Corpus Christi, second Thursday after Whitsun Ascension day (*Asensión*) 40 days after Easter
15 August	Assumption of the Virgin (*Asunción*)
12 October	Virgin of Pilar
8 December	Immaculate Conception (*Inmaculada Concepción*)
25 December	Christmas (*Navidad*)

Appendix 6:
Further reading

A search of Amazon UK gives a substantial number of books relating to Spain, including the following.

Hampshire, David (2003) *Living and Working in Spain*, Survival Books, Fleet

Hampshire, David *Buying a Home in Spain*, Survival Books, Fleet

Howell *et al* (2002) *Buying a Property in Spain*, Cadogan

King, Harry (2002) *Buying a Property in Spain*, How to Books, Oxford

Richards, Robert A C (1998) *Living and Working in Spain*, How to Books, Oxford

Searl, David (2003) *You and the Law in Spain*, Santana Books

Styles, Joanna (2002) *The Best Places to Buy a Home in Spain*, Survival Books, Fleet

The book by David Searl is particularly useful for those already living in Spain, though it is not light reading at nearly 400 pages, and retails at about £20.

Index

Index

Index of advertisers

Also available from Kogan Page in *The Complete Guide to ...* series:

The Complete Guide to Buying and Renting Your First Home
Niki Chesworth

The Complete Guide to Buying and Selling Property
second edition, Sarah O'Grady

The Complete Guide to Buying Property Abroad
second edition, Liz Hodgkinson

The Complete Guide to Buying Property in France
second edition, Charles Davey

The Complete Guide to Buying Property in Italy
Barbara McMahon

The Complete Guide to Letting Property
second edition, Liz Hodgkinson

The Complete Guide to Renovating and Improving Your Property
Liz Hodgkinson

The above titles are available from all good bookshops. To obtain further information, please contact the publisher at the address below:

Kogan Page
120 Pentonville Road
London N1 9JN
Tel:020 7278 0433
Fax:020 7837 6348
www.kogan-page.co.uk